The HITTITES

J. G. Macqueen

The HITTITES
and their contemporaries in Asia Minor

Revised and enlarged edition

WITH 149 ILLUSTRATIONS, MAPS AND PLANS

THAMES AND HUDSON

Ancient Peoples and Places
GENERAL EDITOR: GLYN DANIEL

For Sandra
luce mihi dilectior

© 1975 and 1986 Thames and Hudson Ltd, London

This revised edition first published in the USA in 1986 by
Thames and Hudson Inc., 500 Fifth Avenue,
New York, New York 10110

Library of Congress Catalog Card Number 85-51750

Printed and bound in the German Democratic Republic

Contents

Preface

It is only in the fairly recent past that the Hittites have emerged from the obscurity which had enveloped them for almost three thousand years. Until the nineteenth century, knowledge of them was confined to a few references in the Old Testament, most of which numbered them among the many minor tribes of the hill-country of Palestine. But one or two passages implied something more important than this: that the 'Kings of the Hittites' were rulers of a powerful military people, and that their kingdom lay somewhere to the north of Israel. This was confirmed by the decipherment of Egyptian and Assyrian records which showed that in northern Syria in the years between about 1500 and 700 BC these countries were in contact with – and often in opposition to – a people who were unmistakably the northern Hittites of the Old Testament. In the early years of the twentieth century it became clear from archaeological work, which included the discovery of thousands of texts, that the centre of their power, at least in the second millennium BC, was not in Syria but in north-central Anatolia; and that the 'Kings of the Hittites' were no minor tribal chieftains, but rather the rulers of one of the Great Powers of the ancient Middle East. For several hundred years they played a major part in the 'power game' of their times, and their success in achieving a balance with the other powers was a principal factor in the prosperity and stability, not only of Anatolia, but of much of the contemporary civilized world. It is therefore clear that if we want to have any understanding of that world as a whole, and perhaps to learn from it something of the workings and of the dangers of power-politics, both ancient and modern, we must look to our knowledge of the Hittites as well as that of better-known powers such as Egypt and Assyria.

But there is more to it than that. The records of the Hittites, and the material remains of the communities in which they lived, have far more to tell us than the details of their military campaigns and political intrigues. By studying them we can see the Hittites as people, and observe the way they lived and thought about their lives. The palaces and houses which they occupied, the temples and shrines in which they worshipped, the texts which they wrote, the works of art which they produced and the household utensils which they used – all these help us to see them as it were in the round, as human beings rather than as inanimate pieces in a game of political chess.

Although the Hittites play the leading role in this book, I have tried also to bring in whenever possible information on their Anatolian neighbours. On all sides of the Hittite homeland there were other kingdoms, large and small, with whom the Hittites had necessarily to deal before their international pretensions could be transformed into reality. Excavations at sites in these areas have greatly extended our knowledge of many different areas of Anatolia in the Hittite period. Unfortunately no written records, other than those of the Hittites, have as yet emerged to supplement the archaeological evidence. Such records are known to have existed, and when and if they are found they will greatly enlarge our knowledge of these other kingdoms, and of their relations with the Hittite state and with other areas of the Middle Eastern and Aegean world.

One problem which any writer on the ancient Middle East must face is that of chronology. Many of the dates which have been established for the area are ultimately dependent on Egyptian sources, and professional Egyptologists have a habit, baffling to the outsider but necessary because of the complexity of their material, of revising their chronology either upwards or downwards on an almost annual basis. In the first edition of this book I made use of the Egyptian dates given in the third edition (1970) of the Cambridge Ancient History, the standard work on the period. Since then a downward shift of about twenty-five years has become widely accepted. But final settlement of chronological problems is as far away as ever, and it is with some hesitation that I have used lower dates in this edition. They will, however, if nothing else, bring the book into greater harmony with other volumes in the 'Ancient Peoples and Places' series.

It must indeed be clear that no book of this nature can entirely avoid dealing with problems. There are always many topics on which widely differing views are held, and many too on which the evidence is insufficient, or too ambiguous, to admit of an easy or certain solution. In writing this book I have found myself expressing views and offering reconstructions with which others will undoubtedly disagree. But I have tried at all times to preserve a clear distinction between established fact and personal opinion, and to provide references to works where differing viewpoints may be found. In this way I hope that readers will be able to see through my personal bias to a clearer view of what is much more important and much more interesting – the Hittites themselves and their Anatolian neighbours.

I would like to express my warmest thanks to Gordon Kelsey, Martyn Williams and David Roberts for photographic work; to Elizabeth Induni for artwork; to Jeanne Bishop and Jeanine Erskine for faultless typing and hot water for coffee; to Edmund Lee and Pandora Hay for supplying photographs; to generations of Bristol University students for stimulating discussion and for making obvious the many defects in the first edition; and to my wife and family for putting up with the Hittites for so long.

J.G.M.

1 View from the King's
Gate, Boğazköy. The
photograph shows the
typically bare central
Anatolian hill-country which
lies south of the capital. In
Hittite times much of it
must have been thickly
wooded.

1
Background and environment

The area which we know as Anatolia or Asia Minor is part of the great 2 mountain-system which extends from beyond the Himalayas to the Atlantic seaboard of France, Spain and North Africa. It consists of a high central plateau of ancient rock averaging about three thousand feet above sea-level, and limited to north and south by the geologically newer folds of the Pontus and Taurus Mountains. The whole forms a huge peninsula thrusting out between the Black Sea and the Mediterranean, and sloping gradually down from the Armenian mountains in the east until its rocky ridges extend out into and finally disappear under the waters of the Aegean Sea.

Bordering as it does on Syria and Mesopotamia to the south-east, and on Europe to the north-west, Anatolia has inevitably been an area which has seen many incursions of peoples and many changes of government. But it would be wrong to think of it merely as a 'land bridge' between Asia and Europe. The peoples who were attracted to Anatolia did not come merely because it was a convenient short cut, but because it was a land of rich possibilities, a source of important raw materials that made it a primary centre rather than a backwater which served only to link more favoured areas. This is the case equally in the later second millennium BC, which will be our main concern in the present volume, and in many other periods of its long history. Ionia, for instance, was the area in which what we think of as Greek civilization first grew up. For the Romans, the province of Asia was one of the richest of their empire, and ultimately they recognized that the centre of political, cultural and economic gravity was far to the east of Italy, and moved their capital to Constantinople, a city which, through not actually in Anatolia, is only a mile or two away across the straits.

What was the attraction of Anatolia? It was, first of all, a rich source of timber and agricultural products of all kinds. This is difficult to believe when one looks at the arid, treeless steppe-country of central 1 Anatolia today, but the more fertile coastal regions and the sheltered valleys of the interior give some idea of what much of the country must have been like before the destruction of trees by goats and timber-hungry humans, followed by centuries of neglect, reduced it to its present state. Certainly the presence of large and numerous ancient settlements in areas such as that to the south of the central Salt Lake which are now semi-desert, is an indication that conditions were very different in ancient times.

Black Sea

İstanbul

S. of Marmara

İzmit

Eflanı
Kastamo
Safranb

Gerede
Bolu
Ilgaz

İznik

Çank

Bursa
L. Apolyont
Dorak

Inegöl

İnand
Bitik

R. Sakarya

Beypazarı

Ilıca

Ankara

Kumtepe
Troy

Balıkesir

Eskişehir
Porsuk Çay

Gordion

Polatlı

Gâvurkal

Tavşanlı

Kütahya

Lesbo
Thermi

Akhısar

Afyon

Salt
Lake

Manisa
Sipylus
Sardis

İzmir
Karabel

Klazomenai

Kusura
Beycesultan

L. Eğridir

Ilgın

Ephesus

Büyük Menderes

Aphrodisias

L. Beyşehir
Fassılar

Konya
Karahüyük

Miletus

L. Burdur
Lake District

Eflatun
Pınar

Çatal H.

Iasos

Hacılar

Can Hasan

Müsgebi

Karaman

Antalya

Rhodes

Kaş

Cape Gelidonya

Cyprus

▲ Ancient sites and monuments

• Modern towns

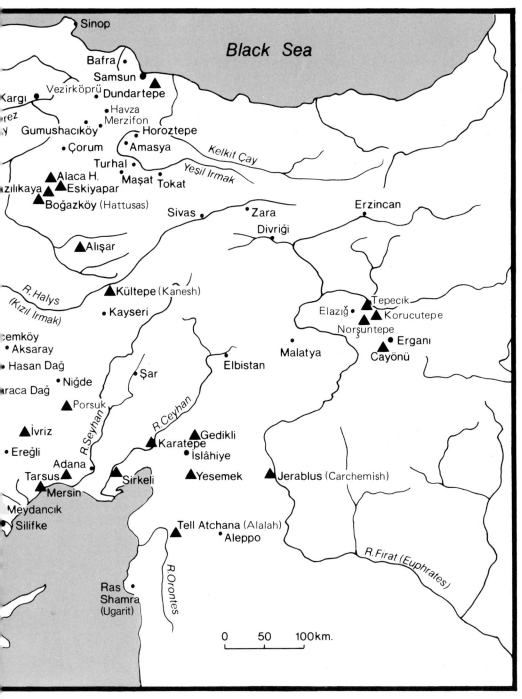

Sinop

Black Sea

Bafra

Samsun

Vezirköprü Dundartepe

Kargı

rez

y Gumushacıköy

Havza
Merzifon

Horoztepe

Çorum

Amasya

Kelkit Çay

Turhal

Yeşil Irmak

Alaca H.

Maşat Tokat

zılıkaya Eskiyapar

Boğazköy (Hattusas)

Sivas

Zara

Erzincan

Divriği

Alışar

R. Halys

(Kızıl Irmak)

Kültepe (Kanesh)

Kayseri

Tepecık

Elazığ

Korucutepe

Norşuntepe

emköy
Aksaray

Ergani

Malatya

Cayönü

Hasan Dağ

Şar

Elbistan

Niğde

raca Dağ

Porsuk

İvriz

Gedikli

Karatepe

Ereğli

İslâhiye

Adana

Tarsus

Sirkeli

Yesemek

Jerablus (Carchemish)

Mersin

Meydancık

Silifke

Tell Atchana (Alalah)

Aleppo

R. Firat (Euphrates)

R.Seyhan

R.Ceyhan

R.Orontes

Ras
Shamra
(Ugarit)

0   50   100km.

2 Map of present-day Anatolia. Known ancient names are given in brackets.

But agricultural wealth alone cannot account for the attraction of Anatolia. It was no more fertile than other areas whose inhabitants were drawn towards it. What they were looking for, and what Anatolia could provide for them, was an abundance of the mineral wealth which with the advance of civilization became increasingly necessary. The mountains of Anatolia are rich in metal-deposits, and it will be suggested in the course of our narrative that metalliferous areas were of great economic and political importance in the history of the ancient Middle East.

Neolithic Anatolia

In recent years it has become clear that Anatolia was an area of vital importance in human development in the Neolithic period, even before the development of metalworking. The discovery that animals and crops could be domesticated, which was first made in the Middle East between 9000 and 7000 BC, has been described as a 'Neolithic Revolution', but its importance lies not so much in its immediate effect (the establishment of settled agricultural villages) as in its enormous potential as a basis for further advance, given the right stimulus and the right conditions. An agricultural village does not grow automatically into a town, but one result of its formation is an increased demand for materials, such as flint and obsidian, which are necessary to make cultivating-tools and other equipment. At the same time it makes its inhabitants much less mobile than their hunting forbears and so less able to find these materials for themselves. In this way trade becomes increasingly important, and those communities which happen to have vital materials on their doorsteps are in a position which they can exploit to the full. Such communities can rapidly increase in wealth and in size, for agriculture provides not only the stimulus for their advance but also the economic basis on which it can be founded. It need hardly be added that this is not the only way in which communities can increase – in southern Mesopotamia, for instance, a main stimulus appears to have been a lack of raw materials rather than a monopoly of them – but a community of the type described has been partially excavated at Çatal Hüyük in the Konya Plain in southern Anatolia. This Neolithic town covers an area of 32 acres, and is by far the largest site of its age so far found. It was occupied from before 7000 BC until about 5600 BC, and it is reasonably assumed that its precocious development was based not only on a prosperous agricultural and pastoral economy, made possible by the exceptional conditions offered by the gradual drying-up of a pluvial lake in what is now the Konya Plain, but also on the community's exploitation of the obsidian which was obtained from the near-by volcanoes of the Hasan Dağ and Karaca Dağ. A wall-painting which has been preserved has been interpreted by the excavator as a view of the town with an eruption of Hasan Dağ in the background. Surface survey-work on sites nearer Hasan Dağ has shown the presence of Neolithic remains, earlier than those of Çatal Hüyük and clearly connected with obsidian-working, and it is possible that further sites like Çatal Hüyük will be found in other obsidian-producing areas – eastern Anatolia, for instance – if the agricultural

3

3 Wall-painting from Çatal Hüyük, perhaps showing volcanic eruption with town in foreground. *c.* 6200 BC (after Mellaart).

potential proves to have been sufficiently high to support them. No such sites are yet known, but there is evidence for the 'export' of eastern Anatolian obsidian to the Zagros area, on the borders of Iraq and Iran, as early as *c.* 30,000 BC.

Though their prosperity was based on obsidian, the inhabitants of Çatal Hüyük were also acquainted with the use of other local materials which were to be of infinitely greater value in the later history of Anatolia. Already before 7000 BC at Çayönü, close to the rich Ergani Maden copper-mines near modern Elazığ, native copper was being cold-hammered into tools and pins, and there are signs of heat being used in a quenching process. Before 6000 BC local smiths at Çatal Hüyük had mastered the technique of smelting, and were producing copper and lead beads and other small trinkets.

Slowly methods of production and workmanship were improved, and the use of metal spread from its original mountain home (or homes: other areas, such as Iran, must have had an equal part to play) into the plains of Mesopotamia, where metal objects, previously very rare, played an increasingly important part in the Tell Halaf culture[1] – a culture which has clear northern connections, and may ultimately be linked with contemporary cultures somewhere in Anatolia. From this time on, the Anatolian mountains were always a principal source of metals and of metallurgical techniques to the Mesopotamian world.

It is unfortunate that developments in metallurgy are so often difficult to follow because of lack of evidence. Unlike scrap pottery, scrap metal can be, and normally is, melted down for re-use, and it is only by chance that specimens survive. Often the only way in which one can tell what the metal vessels of a particular period looked like is to study the shapes of the pottery which was made and even coloured to imitate metal. In a few instances the discovery of 'royal' tombs in which metal vessels and implements are preserved yields information of far greater value than that of the gold and silver found. But such tombs as have so far been discovered date from a much later period.

The Chalcolithic and Early Bronze Ages

With the increased importance of metals and metal technology, the north-central and north-western parts of Anatolia, which contained rich metal-deposits, were increasingly developed, and settlements began to grow and prosper.[2] But it is worthwhile mentioning that they grew in their own characteristic way, a way quite unlike that of areas such as Egypt and Mesopotamia where conditions and stimuli were

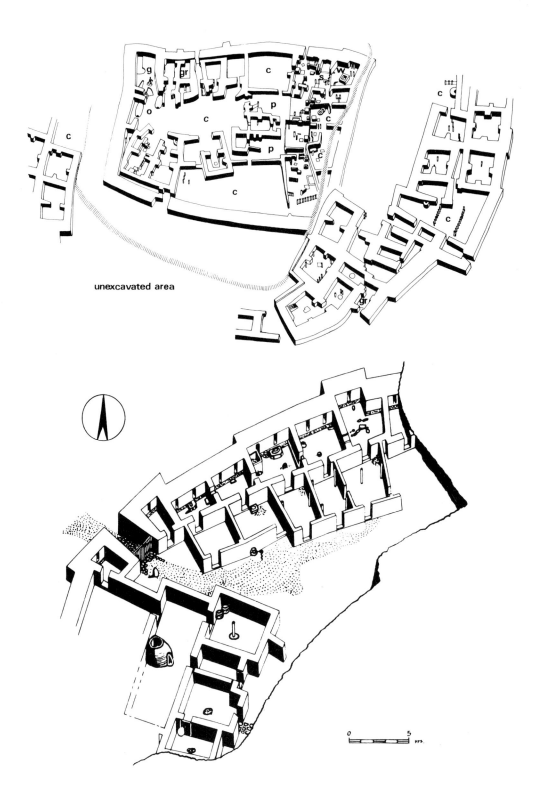

unexcavated area

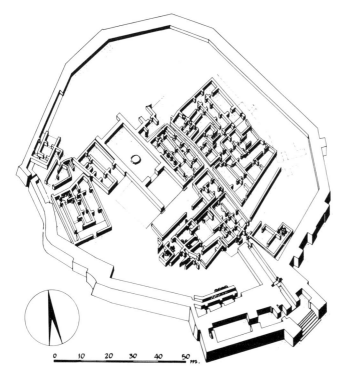

4 Isometric view of Hacılar
II–I, *c.* 5400–5250 BC:
c courtyard; *g* granary;
gr guardroom; *p* potters
workshops; *w* well; *s* shrine
(after Mellaart).

5 Isometric view of Mersin
XVI citadel, *c.* 4000 BC (after
Lloyd).

6 Reconstructed plan of
Troy II citadel, *c.* 2300 BC
(after Lloyd).

different. In southern Mesopotamia for instance the settlements grew
up around temples, and the temple with its lofty tower became a central
feature.[3] But in Anatolia we can glimpse something else happening.
The best illustration of this is perhaps the little settlement of Hacılar in
the 'Lake District' of southern Turkey. In the years before about 5400
BC Hacılar had, apart from an attractive pottery-style, little to
distinguish it from other contemporary agricultural villages in the
Middle East. But about 5400 a rectangular area measuring *c.* 57 × 36.5
m was cut off and fortified by an enclosure wall of mud brick. Inside
this fortification were a granary, potters' workshops, a well and a small
shrine. Clearly the local ruler had constructed a rudimentary fortress
for the safety and comfort of himself and his followers. After the
destruction of this castle another larger one was built on the same site,
and it is possible to see in these structures the beginning of something
that was to be characteristic of the Anatolian-Aegean area at a later
period – the fortified citadel. The outline of the development can be
seen in what looks like a section of a similar structure at Can Hasan, just
north of the Taurus, and then at Mersin in Cilicia, where one can see
the rooms inside the wall with their slit-windows overlooking the
country below, the piles of sling-stones made ready for action, and the
'commander's residence' alongside the narrow entrance. Later still, in
the third millennium BC, the fortified citadel can be seen in both central
and western Anatolia. The same essential pattern is to be found in
Greece as early as about 3000 BC, at the site of Dimini in Thessaly. Its
survival in the citadels of Mycenaean and Classical Greece, and its
ultimate introduction by the Crusaders to western Europe, are subjects
which are beyond the scope of this book.

4

5

6

To return to Anatolia, the area seems by the latter part of the third millennium BC to have become a land of small city-states, their rulers living in castles, their economies based primarily on agriculture, but their real wealth and importance residing in their metals and metal products. Examples of these products are to be seen in the 'treasures' of Alaca Hüyük and other sites in north-central Anatolia, and of Troy in the north-west. Similar finds have been acquired by Western museums and collectors.[4] These treasures are of comparatively late date (say 2300 BC for Troy and 2200 for Alaca,[5] but the advanced nature of the techniques employed makes it certain that they are the products of a long tradition of metalworking. Although their relationship to the equally famous treasures of Maikop, north of the Caucasus,[6] and Ur in southern Mesopotamia[7] has yet to be fully worked out, it can be claimed that the Anatolian works are not mere derivatives from another area – certainly not from the more 'civilized' south-east. There has in fact been a feeling among some Mesopotamian archaeologists that the Ur treasures are intrusive there, brought by some foreign dynasty from the north. This would certainly be in keeping with the earlier patterns of influence noted above.

So Anatolia in the period which is known to archaeologists as 'Early Bronze II' (c. 2600–2300 BC) was in a commanding position. It had both the resources that were necessary for a Bronze Age economy and the techniques needed to exploit them. Thus, it had an important part to play in the Middle Eastern world, and its connections can be seen to have spread out as far as south Russia and southern Mesopotamia. To the metal-less rulers of Mesopotamia it must have been of particular importance, and so we find it included in the many areas to which they dispatched their merchants. Legend (though not yet archaeology) tells of the activities of merchants sent out about 2300 BC by the kings of Akkad to the town of Purushanda, which probably lay south of the central Salt Lake and may well be identified with the rich site of Acem Hüyük near Aksaray. If the identification is correct, firm evidence may soon be forthcoming from the excavations now being carried out there. In the meantime, partial confirmation of the existence of the trade is to be found at the site of Tell Brak,[8] on the caravan-route from northern Mesopotamia to Anatolia, where Naram-Sin of Akkad built an elaborate palace in the ruins of which were discovered several imports from Anatolia.

7 Bull-figure from Horoztepe, c. 2200 BC. H. 41 cm.

8 Bull-figure from Maikop, c. 2200 BC.

Assyrian merchant-colonies

The destruction of the empire of Akkad by barbarian invasions led to the interruption of this trade, but by about 1940 BC merchants from Assyria were to be found at several towns in Anatolia, notably at Kanesh, modern Kültepe near Kayseri, where extensive excavations in the *karum* or trading-quarter have revealed not only the houses of these merchants but also large quantities of their business correspondence written on tablets of clay. From these records we can see what the principal articles of trade were, and perhaps deduce both the importance of Anatolia at the time and the difficulties that were to influence political policy throughout the second millennium. The

Assyrians clearly wanted silver, gold and copper, and what they gave in exchange was woollen cloth, made-up clothing of various types, and a metal which despite much argument is almost certainly tin rather than lead.[9] In this trade it is tempting to see both the reasons for the prosperity of the Anatolians and the principal difficulty they had in maintaining that prosperity. For Anatolia, although it is rich in minerals and has plentiful supplies of copper, is comparatively poor in tin. There are some small deposits, but nothing like enough to supply the needs of a full Bronze Age economy. Where the Assyrians got their tin from is by no means clear (the question of tin-sources will be more fully discussed in Chapter 3). But whatever its origin, the Anatolians were eager to have it. So a largely peaceful relationship developed between the local communities and the Assyrian merchants, who lived in Anatolian houses, used Anatolian equipment, and often, if we can trust the evidence of proper names, took Anatolian wives. In fact, were it not for the language of the documents it would often be impossible to detect 'Assyrian' influence at all, and some of the best evidence for one of the richest and finest periods of Anatolian craftsmanship is to be found in the houses of the Assyrian merchants. Other sites, such as Hattus at modern Boğazköy, Acem Hüyük mentioned above, and Karahüyük near Konya also attest the prosperity of central Anatolia at

9 Ritual vases in form of lions from Kültepe. Av. H. 20 cm. These vessels, and the jug shown in ill. 10, illustrate the high quality of Anatolian craftsmanship at the time of the Assyrian merchant-colonies (the Colony period).

10 Beak-spouted jugs from Kültepe. H. *c.* 40 cm.

this time. In the south-west too there are signs of equal prosperity at Beycesultan, where a large palace and other public buildings on a grand scale have been excavated, while in the north-west Troy was beginning to recover from a period of comparative decline and would soon take its place once more as an important site. These areas too presumably had their sources of tin (other metals were amply available), but it is at present not clear what they were. A possible source will be suggested below.

After the merchant-colonies

About 1780 BC, for reasons which are not yet completely clear but which are probably connected with political and ethnic movements in Mesopotamia, the Assyrian trade-connection with central Anatolia came to an abrupt end. The Hurrians, a people of unknown affiliations whose original homeland seems to have been in the region of Lake Urmia and who had for many years been spreading across northern Mesopotamia towards the Mediterranean Sea, had by now begun to achieve political supremacy in the states on the upper Tigris and Euphrates and in the hills bordering on south-east Anatolia. This meant that Assyria was cut off from her commercial colonies, and her power quickly collapsed. Soon she was incorporated into the expanding empire of Hammurabi of Babylon.

For the Anatolians, the loss of the Assyrian connection was a disastrous blow. On the whole, the cities that flourished during the period of the Assyrian merchant-colonies went into a decline from which they never recovered, and as Hurrian pressure built up to the east the situation grew more serious. Not only Assyria, but the routes through the Anti-Taurus were lost. The only alternative available to the central Anatolians was the route running down through Cilicia, across to the Euphrates, and on to southern Mesopotamia. We have little contemporary information on this route, but that it too was a tin-route, and that it had connections with Kanesh, can be seen from the archives of Mari on the middle Euphrates. The trouble with it was that it was in the hands of powerful kingdoms – Babylon in the south, Mari in the centre, and Aleppo in the north. Yet tin must still have been a necessity, and inevitably the interests of the central Anatolians were drawn towards the Euphrates-route and the dangerous ground of Middle Eastern politics.

During the last years of the Assyrian trading-colonies the dominating position in central Anatolian affairs had been seized by the rulers of the state of Kussara, a city which is often said to have been in central Anatolia, but which was more probably situated further to the east, in the area around modern Divriği, near one of the routes from Assyria. Pithanas, the first recorded ruler of this state, extended his influence to Nesas (more accurately Neshash), which may well be an alternative spelling of Kanesh in an attempt to represent an original Knesh (developing in the same way as the English 'knee') with the addition of a nominal suffix -as. His son Anittas soon transferred the capital to Nesas, and proceeded to extend his conquests to other central Anatolian principalities including Hattus, which he destroyed and declared accursed. By the end of his life (*c.* 1750 BC) he had acquired a sufficiently substantial kingdom to claim the title of 'great king'. Unfortunately our documentary evidence fails us at this point, and it is impossible to say what happened to the kingdom of Anittas. In a large burnt building at Kanesh a spearhead has been discovered bearing the inscription 'palace of Anita, the king', and the building may also, for all we know, have contained the burnt remains of its ruler. Who the destroyers were is a matter of guesswork – one plausible suggestion is that they came from the state of Zalpa, near the Black Sea coast in the region of modern Bafra. But when the picture becomes clearer again, about a hundred years later, we find a ruler who claims that his origin is in Kussara setting up his capital at Hattus (or Hattusas as it is now called), and to celebrate the event changing his name to Hattusilis. Whatever his connection with the earlier rulers – and in view of his flouting of the curse it may not have been a particularly close one – this is the monarch who was the founder of what we know as the Hittite kingdom.

11

11 Spear-head found at Kültepe, with inscription reading 'Palace of Anita, the king'. The bent tang has been broken, and the two holes through which the head was bound to the shaft have apparently been wrongly placed, filled in, and remade further down. L. 23 cm.

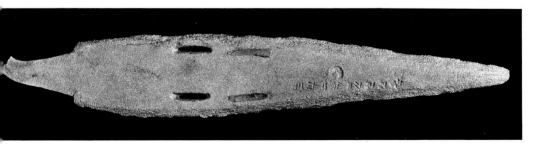

2

Who were the Hittites?

In 1902 the Norwegian scholar J. A. Knudtzon announced to a sceptical world that he had discovered a new Indo-European language. It was to be found, he claimed, written in a cuneiform script on two clay tablets which had been discovered fifteen years earlier at El Amarna in Egypt among the diplomatic correspondence of the pharaohs Akhenaten (*c.* 1367–1351) and his father Amenophis III (*c.* 1405–1367). Since one of the tablets was addressed to the king of a hitherto unknown country called Arzawa, the language was named Arzawan. Knudtzon's suggestion of an Indo-European connection, though plausible, found little favour with his contemporaries, but it was known that a few fragments of tablets written in the same language had been found at Boğazköy in central Anatolia, and excavations begun there in 1906 soon brought to light an archive of thousands of tablets, many of which were written in 'Arzawan'. There was now ample material for a full linguistic study, the result of which, as announced by B. Hrozný in 1915, was a full confirmation of Knudtzon's claim. The language of the texts was indeed basically Indo-European, and so gave scholars their earliest surviving evidence for a member of that linguistic family.

Important as this discovery was for the philologists, for the historians it brought many problems. Central Anatolia was scarcely the place where they had expected to find early speakers of Indo-European, and they had to ask themselves firstly who these people were, and in the second place how and when they had got there. Fortunately, the first question was easily answered. The tablets themselves showed quite clearly that Boğazköy was ancient Hattusas, the capital of the land of Hatti and the seat of rulers who had, during the fourteenth and thirteenth centuries BC, been among the most important of the Middle Eastern world. Obviously the language of the tablets was that of the kings of Hatti. It was consequently re-christened 'Hittite', and the name 'Arzawan' was quietly forgotten.

Identifying the Hittites

But the solution to this problem raised other problems which demanded answers. It had in fact been suspected for some time that Boğazköy was the capital of the Hittites, but the grounds for this identification seemed to be contradicted by the new evidence. In 1876 A. H. Sayce had suggested that certain basalt blocks inscribed with a

12 Inscription in 'Hieroglyphic Hittite' from Hamath (after Messerschmidt).

hieroglyphic script and found at Aleppo and Hamath in northern Syria were in fact the work of the Hittites, a people hitherto known only from references in the Bible and in the records of Egypt and Assyria. In 1880 Sayce further suggested that a number of rock carvings in south-east, central and western Asia Minor, some of which were associated with the same script as appeared on the Syrian blocks, were also of Hittite workmanship. By 1900 almost a hundred 'Hittite' inscribed monuments of this sort had been recorded. Among these was one which stood in a prominent position among the ruins of Boğazköy, and the natural conclusion was that the site was that of a large and important Hittite city. Consequently it was rather a shock to discover that Hittite records were written in a cuneiform script, for if 'Arzawan' was really Hittite, who wrote in the hieroglyphic script? The issue was complicated by the fact that although the basic decipherment of the cuneiform texts proved to be fairly simple, the hieroglyphic texts were a much more difficult matter. Still, patient work by several scholars succeeded in resolving a large number of their problems, and the

12

14, 15

13

13 Hieroglyphic inscription, much worn, Nişantaş, Boğazköy.

14 Rock relief at Karabel, east of Izmir. This relief has been taken to be a monument of Hittite conquest in the west, but is more probably the work of a local king.

discovery of a long bilingual inscription in 1947 provided confirmation for much of their work and a great increase in the understanding of the script and language. 'Hieroglyphic Hittite' is also an Indo-European language. Most of the known texts can now be seen to date from a period after the fall of the Hittite kingdom, and are the work of south-east Anatolian and north Syrian monarchs who preserved the name and tradition of the old Hittite realm; but some texts go back to the hey-day of the Hittite Empire and are the work of known Hittite monarchs. Yet the language of these inscriptions, while fairly closely related to that of the cuneiform texts, is by no means identical with it. Clearly both languages existed side by side in the Hittite realms, with 'Hieroglyphic Hittite' gradually playing a larger part. It has been suggested that later Hittite monarchs were 'Hieroglyphic Hittites' who took over the kingdom of the 'cuneiform' Hittites, and it has even been maintained that latterly cuneiform Hittite was a dead language used only through the conservatism of royal scribes. However this may be (and there may well be some truth in it) it seems clear that the hieroglyphic script and language were introduced to the Hittite realms from some outside source at a period preceding the greatest days of the Hittite Empire, perhaps during the second half of the fifteenth century BC.

What was that outside source? 'Hittite Hieroglyphs' were already in use in Cilicia by about 1500 BC, as can be seen from the seal of a king of that area excavated at Tarsus. Another seal found at Beycesultan in south-western Anatolia and securely dated to the twentieth century BC

15 Rock relief at Gavurkalesi near Ankara. Two gods face a seated goddess. Behind the relief lies a tomb-chamber which may once have contained the remains of a local monarch.

bears signs which have been identified by some scholars as 'Hittite Hieroglyphs'. It has therefore been suggested that the home of this script, and of the people who spoke the language written in it, was the southern and south-western part of Asia Minor. The further identification of these peoples is unexpectedly aided by material from the archives of Boğazköy. As well as cuneiform Hittite, several other languages are used in these texts, and one of them is named as Luwian. The curious thing is that 'Hieroglyphic Hittite' is much more closely related to Luwian than it is to cuneiform Hittite, and the two seem in fact to be dialect variants of the same language. But we can go further than this. Luwian is presumably the language of the area known in the cuneiform texts as Luwiya, and Luwiya can be seen to be the earlier name of an area referred to in the Hittite Imperial period as Arzawa. And so we reach the final position that the language originally known as Arzawan is in fact the language of the Hittites, while the language written in 'Hittite Hieroglyphs' is a dialect of the language of Arzawa.

What and where is Arzawa? A study of the Hittite archives serves to show that the group of states known to the Hittites by this name formed the principal power of western Anatolia, with their centre either in the Turkish 'Lake District', or, more probably, in what was later known as Lydia. The part that they had to play in Hittite history will be detailed in a later chapter. Here it is sufficient to say that it is increasingly clear that Arzawa was a powerful state with considerable influence in both Anatolian and international politics, and that if her records were to be

21, 22

recovered they would tell us a great deal that we would like to know about both the Near Eastern and the Aegean worlds.

To return now to our original argument, it can be seen that between 1400 and 1200 BC large parts of Anatolia were controlled by speakers of Indo-European languages. The north-central area, centred on Hattusas, was the heartland of the Hittites, while the areas south and west of this were occupied by speakers of Luwian and the closely related dialect originally known as 'Hieroglyphic Hittite', but now usually called 'Anatolian Hieroglyphic' or 'Hieroglyphic Luwian'. The history of these peoples has been reconstructed with a fair degree of detail from their surviving records, and so the first question raised above – the identity of those who wrote the texts – can be given a reasonably full answer.

Hittite origins

But the second question remains to be answered. The evidence for the original 'homeland' of the Indo-European languages seems to be overwhelmingly against a situation in Anatolia, and this means that speakers of an Indo-European language must have entered Anatolia at some time and from some other area. But from what area? And at what time? On the first point there is now fairly general agreement that the linguistic evidence points to an Indo-European 'homeland' somewhere in the area that stretches from the lower Danube along the north shore of the Black Sea to the northern foot-hills of the Caucasus. In that area it has plausibly been connected with the archaeological culture known as *Kurgan*, the bearers of which spread originally from the Eurasian steppes, reaching the Black Sea towards the end of the fifth millennium, and by the third millennium penetrating much of Europe from the Baltic to the Aegean.[10] The culture is typified by tumuli (*kurgans*) covering burials in house-type graves, often richly endowed with funeral gifts. If this is accepted, it seems virtually certain that speakers of an Indo-European language must have reached Anatolia from the north, and the only question to be settled is whether they came from the north-west, via the Dardanelles and the Bosporus, or from the north-east, via the passes of the Caucasus.[11] On this issue scholarly opinion has been fairly evenly divided, and it is necessary to turn from linguistic to archaeological evidence. Attempts to link change of language to changes that are archaeologically recognizable are potentially dangerous, and have been roundly condemned by both linguists and archaeologists.[12] It is however difficult to believe that a new language can be successfully introduced to an area without material change of any kind. At any rate the hypothesis of 'no linguistic change without archaeological change' is one that in the absence of linguistic evidence we are forced to adopt if we are not to abandon hope of solving the problem. Extreme caution is of course required, and if the hypothesis is seen to be contradicted at any point by the linguistic evidence which is available, it must be abandoned at once. But if the linguistic and archaeological evidence are seen to complement one another there is a reasonable chance that the hypothesis may lead towards the truth.

Archaeological evidence

In examining the archaeological evidence from Anatolia it is perhaps best to start in the south-west, where we have seen reason to suppose that there were Indo-European-speakers between 1400 and 1200 BC, with a possibility that they were already there by 2000 BC. Certainly between these two dates there is no sign of an archaeological break at Beycesultan, the principal excavated site for this area, and this helps to confirm the scanty linguistic evidence from the site. But a little earlier than this, at the end of the period known as Beycesultan XIII, there are considerable signs of destruction, and the following level, Beycesultan XII, shows clear signs of change. The new culture, which continued without interruption until the end of the Bronze Age, can be seen to be related in its origins to the culture of the second city of Troy, in north-west Anatolia. This Trojan culture has also many links with the Cilician culture known as EB III. These links have been variously interpreted. Troy II has been regarded as the ancestor of Cilician EB III, and the two have also been seen as being contemporary. On the whole, it seems more probable that there is in fact an overlap between them.[13] Cilician EB III has sufficient connection with cultures further east and south to establish a fairly accurate date for it, and it seems to have lasted from about 2400 to 2000 BC. This gives us a date of perhaps 2200 BC for the end of Troy II and, since there are elements of Troy II, III and IV in Beycesultan XII–VIII, c. 2300 BC is a reasonable date for the introduction of the north-western culture to the south-west. If then we may claim that this culture was brought by speakers of an Indo-European language, then this language must have been spoken in north-west Anatolia during the Troy II period, and have reached there from south-eastern Europe at some time early in or before that period. But although both Troy IIa and Troy I were destroyed (c. 2500 and c. 2600 BC), there is no sign at either time of any intrusive cultural element from Europe. There is a similar lack of new elements at the beginning of Troy I (c. 2900 BC?) and even during the preceding Kumtepe Ib period, which takes us back to at least 3000 BC. It has to be admitted, in fact, that the trail cannot at present be followed into south-eastern Europe, and that there are few obvious signs of any *Kurgan* penetration into north-western Anatolia. But the fortified settlement of Troy itself   6 is comparable in siting and defences to *Kurgan* hill-forts in the Balkans and possibly as far afield as southern Russia,[14] and one can perhaps see in a carved stone block found in secondary use in a middle Troy I   16 context and bearing a strong resemblance to funeral stelae of a type which often marked *Kurgan* burials, an indication that such a   17 movement was already by that time a thing of the past.

Once arrived in Anatolia, the newcomers' progress can be roughly traced. At first they were content to build up the prosperity of the north-west along local lines, but by about 2600 BC they had reached as far inland as Beycesultan, sacking level XVIIa and introducing a culture of Troy I type. The destruction of Troy Ij, followed by that of Troy IIa, proved only a temporary set-back, and shortly after 2500 the Trojans were sufficiently secure and prosperous to take up trading with distant lands. Contact with Cilicia, presumably by sea, can be seen in

16 Limestone *stele*, Troy I.
W. 63 cm.

the introduction of the potter's wheel to the north-west during phase
IIb. About 2400 BC the attraction of Cilicia proved so strong that it was
largely 'taken over' by north-west Anatolians (not just 'Trojans': the
cultures are by no means identical), and Cilicia proved so much more
convenient as a trading-centre that the north-west, as represented by
Troy II d–g, began to lose its importance. Meanwhile Cilicia continued
to prosper, and Cilician influence spread up through the Taurus passes
and on to the southern and south-western parts of the plateau, where it
18   can be seen in pottery shapes at Beycesultan (level XIII). But the
people of Troy II, their overseas expansion thwarted, began to expand
inland once more, and by 2300 BC they had reached and destroyed
Beycesultan, and pushed on across the Konya Plain to the foot-hills of
the Taurus. The over-all result of these conquests, however, was
disastrous. Troy itself could not take advantage of them, for *c.* 2200 it
was itself destroyed by fire, without apparently the involvement of any
outside enemy. In the rest of western and southern Anatolia the over-
all impression is that of a grave decline in material culture. While some
areas recovered within two or three hundred years, others, like Lycia
and Pisidia, seem to have had little settled occupation until the first
millennium.

The invasion seems to have spent its strength before it reached
Cilicia. In this area there is no change of culture until about 2000 BC,
when an intrusive style of painted pottery, often linked with the arrival
of the Hurrians, makes its appearance from northern Syria. But an
unexpected echo of the Indo-European incursions is perhaps to be
found in the legends of the Mesopotamian Dynasty of Akkad.[15] Sargon,
the principal monarch of this dynasty, is said in an admittedly late text

to have made an expedition about 2300 BC in support of a colony of Mesopotamian merchants settled at Purushanda, and another text, also of later date, refers to the invasion of the Akkadian empire and the destruction of Purushanda by barbarous hordes about 2230 BC. Purushanda is almost certainly to be equated with the Purushattum which is mentioned in later texts from Anatolia, and is most probably situated at Acemköy (Acem Hüyük), south of the central Salt Lake. If then the legends have any historical value, they imply Akkadian influence through Cilicia and well up on to the central Anatolian plateau. If this is so, we can perhaps see the spread of Cilician influence in the same direction between 2400 and 2300, as mentioned above, taking place in conjunction with the spread of Akkadian merchant-colonies. The barbarous hordes of the later attacks could then be identified with the spread of Indo-European-speakers from the north-west reaching the Konya Plain by about 2230.

22

The north-central area

The foregoing scheme may perhaps account for the 'Luwianizing' of Anatolia south and west of a line drawn from the Bosporus to the Gulf of Iskenderun. In north-central Anatolia the situation is even more complicated. In this area records in an Indo-European language go back to the earliest days of what we know as the Hittite Old Kingdom, about 1650 BC. Only the 'Anittas-text', which deals with the deeds of the kings of Kussara, refers to events earlier than this, and it may in fact be an Old Kingdom translation into Hittite. Even if it was originally written in Hittite at a time contemporary with the events it describes, this takes us back only to about 1780 BC. The period immediately preceding this, from about 1940 to 1780, is amply documented from the records of the Assyrian merchant-colonists. These records frequently contain names of native Anatolians, and for many years an intensive study has been made of these names with a view to tracing the languages spoken at the time. At first scholarly opinion was inclined to the view that only a few names with an Indo-European etymology were to be found, and that not one of these was unmistakably Hittite. This led to the suggestion that at the period known as Karum II (c. 1940–1840), to which most of the documents belong, the Hittites had not yet reached central Anatolia, and that the destruction of Karum II about 1840 was in fact an indication of their arrival.[16] A line of destruction was traced from the Caucasus to central Anatolia at about the same time, and this was equated with the route taken by the Hittites from the south-Russian steppes. Against this reconstruction there are several objections. First, and most important, further study of the proper names in the Assyrian documents has shown that Indo-European names are much more numerous than was at first supposed, and that many, including a majority of the local rulers' names, can be regarded as 'proto-Hittite'. Second, many archaeologists deny any fundamental break in the archaeological record in Georgia and other areas through which the alleged Hittite invasions must have passed; and third, the linguistic relationship between Hittite and Luwian seems to be too close for one to suppose that they entered Anatolia by such

17 *Kurgan* grave-marker, Natalivka, South Russia. H. 1.62 m (after Gimbutas).

diverse routes. The destruction of Karum II cannot then be accepted as a sign of the arrival of the Hittites. On the contrary, they seem by that time to be already established in a powerful position, and the linguistic evidence can now be seen to agree with what the archaeologists have long been stressing, that central Anatolia in the colony-period is basically Hittite.

What is required then is evidence for a spread of influence to central Anatolia from the areas to the south and west at a period subsequent to the 'Luwianizing' of these areas, but before the colony-period. Archaeologically this spread is easy to observe. Hand-made 'depas' (p. 133) cups at Alişar and Kültepe correspond to those of the so-called 'Trojan' phase in Cilicia; at Kültepe there are also wheel-made plates with the same connection, and grey bottles and other Syrian imports which are likewise common in Cilicia at this time. Other signs may also be observed. The beak-spouted jug, a typically Hittite shape of vessel, is rare in central Anatolia before this period, and it may be suspected that it now appears through the influence of the contemporary culture of south-west Anatolia and Cilicia. Most significant of all is the plan of a large public building at Kültepe. This is in the form of a 'megaron' or hall-and-porch, a type of building which is foreign to central Anatolia but which has a long ancestry in the west.[17] Whether it is to be identified as a temple or a palace, it serves to show that people with western connections had achieved positions of considerable power in the area. The dating of these influences can be roughly linked to the Cilician sequence, and the over-all impression is that this period in central Anatolian prehistory begins about 2350–2300 BC.

One important change in the central Anatolian ceramic repertory has not so far been mentioned. This is the sudden appearance of painted 'Cappadocian' pottery which gives a rather exotic touch to the

18 'Depas' cups. *Top to bottom*: Tarsus EB III, Kültepe EB III, Troy II, Beycesultan XIIIa. Not to scale (after Mellaart).

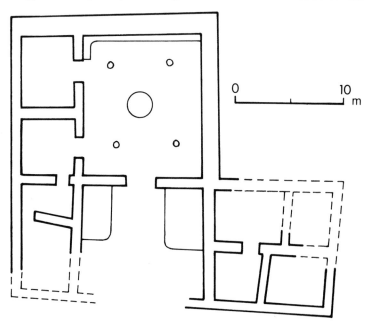

19 Building of megaron type from Kültepe, *c.* 2250 BC (after Lloyd).

predominantly plain tradition of the area. This painted pottery has often been regarded as a Hittite introduction, but it now seems clear that it was a local development from the simpler painted wares of the immediately preceding period. But the spread of Indo-European influence into central Anatolia can perhaps be seen in the fact that early 'Cappadocian' vessels have painted patterns which repeat the incised ornamentation of pottery found at Beycesultan in levels immediately succeeding the 'Luwian' invasion. Thus although the pottery itself is not a Hittite innovation, some features of its development may be linked with the arrival of speakers of an Indo-European language.

One item of linguistic information may also be added. It has been pointed out that the clearly Hittite words išhiul and išpant occur in the records of the Assyrian merchants in connection with the place-names Lawazantiya, Nenassa and Ullama. This suggests that Hittite was spoken in and around these places contemporaneously with the merchant-colonies, and since all three are probably to be located south or south-west of Kültepe we have yet another indication of the direction from which the Indo-Europeanizing movement must have come.

What seems to emerge from all this is a largely peaceful spread of influence – and language – into central Anatolia from the south, and to a lesser extent from the west, shortly after these areas had themselves been 'Indo-Europeanized' from the north-west. The Kültepe megaron shows that the new arrivals had already gained considerable influence there by about 2250, and by the period of the Assyrian merchant-colonies they formed a large proportion of the population, and were clearly even then largely absorbed into the native element. This is only to be expected from the linguistic evidence of the later Hittite texts, where an Indo-European structure is combined with a very large indigenous vocabulary, and from the organization of the Hittite state, which shows no sign of a class-system based on language differences. All this presupposes a long period of previous development with speakers of both Indo-European and non-Indo-European languages present in the population.

At the time of their arrival, the newcomers probably spoke a form of Indo-European that had yet to be differentiated into Hittite, Luwian and other dialects which we know from the later second millennium. For several hundred years Kanesh played the leading part in central Anatolian affairs, but shortly after 1800 the kings of Kussara, a town in the eastern periphery of the area, began to extend their influence westwards. Kanesh and other central towns were conquered, and eventually Kussara was able to take over the dominant position. A hundred years later, as we have seen in chapter 1, rulers in some way connected with Kussara set up their capital at Hattusas, and by this time their language is recognizably a slightly archaic form of Hittite. The script in which they wrote it is not the same as that of the earlier Assyrian colonists, and was presumably adopted by them from some area, as yet unidentified, to the south-east of Anatolia.

The picture that has emerged from the foregoing discussion is a fairly simple one, but it must be said at once that there are complications. The first of these is the fact that there are other signs of western influence on central Anatolia at a slightly later period than the

22

2

22

one described above. About 2000 BC a wheel-made monochrome ware makes its appearance at Kanesh and other central Anatolian sites, and the ancestry of this pottery seems on the evidence of surface surveys to lie in north-west Anatolia, and particularly in the Tavşanlı-Kütahya region. The interesting point about it is that it is to be found in the earliest levels of occupation at Boğazköy, a fact which suggests that the original settlement at this site was made by north-westerners who were presumably Indo-European, but not Hittite, in speech.[18] This drive from the north-west may have been the occasion of the establishment of Palaic, another Indo-European dialect known from the Boğazköy records, in the vicinity of Kastamonu, towards the Black Sea coast north-east of Ankara, the area in which it was probably spoken in the second half of the second millennium. No linguistic features in the Hittite texts from the Boğazköy archives can yet be ascribed to this wave of western influence. It has in fact been claimed that the movement shows the arrival of the Hittites themselves in central Anatolia, but on the whole it seems to be too late and from the wrong direction to satisfy all the evidence.

The Hattians

Another problem which should be mentioned here is that of the predecessors of the Hittites in central Anatolia. The Boğazköy archives contain texts which are described as being in 'Hattic', a language of a completely different structure from Indo-European, and it is usually supposed that the speakers of Hattic were the inhabitants of the land of Hatti before the arrival of the Indo-European-speaking immigrants. If so, they are presumably to be equated with the people of the EB II or 'copper-age' period which immediately preceded the influences described above. This period is well known from Kültepe, Alışar, Alaca and elsewhere, and its most spectacular surviving remains are the 'royal' tombs at Alaca, with their famous 'standards' and other metalwork. But although the ordinary people of the royal tomb period may have spoken Hattic, it is by no means certain that the monarchs who occupied the tombs did so as well. Other slightly later tombs with similar metalwork have been discovered at sites which are closer to the Black Sea coast than Alaca, and it has been suggested that the Alaca tombs show the temporary extension of a northern culture into central Anatolia. Excavations in the northern area are now revealing a good deal more about this northern culture, and it can be seen that its metalwork is in many ways related to that found at Maikop and Tsarkaja in the basin of the Kuban, north of the Caucasus. This Russian culture has reasonably been ascribed to *Kurgan* peoples who had recently come under the influence of higher cultures south of the Caucasus. If so, the occupants of the Alaca tombs, which show many *Kurgan* features, may well also have been *Kurgan* people, speaking an Indo-European language. But there is no sign of any spread of this *Kurgan* culture further south into Anatolia, and so it cannot be linked with the spread of Hittite, to say nothing of Palaic and Luwian. The language of the rulers who were buried in the Alaca tombs, although probably Indo-European, was almost certainly not proto-Hittite.

All of this, of course, brings us no nearer to identifying the Hattians. They *may* have been the peoples of central Anatolia who were temporarily subject to the kings buried at Alaca, and whose remains can also be seen at Alışar and Kültepe, but it has even been suggested that they *followed* the Hittites from south-east Europe into Anatolia rather than preceding them in the central area.[19] It is also worth mentioning that in the records of the Assyrian merchant-colonies the 'Land of Hatti', whose native language one must assume was originally Hattic, may not have been centred on Hattus/Boğazköy, but have been a good deal further to the east, in the area around modern Divriği. The question 'who were the Hattians?' must at present be left open.

Early Greeks in Anatolia

No discussion of the linguistic background to Hittite Anatolia can be complete without some mention of the suggestion that another important group of Indo-European-speakers was to be found there in the late third and throughout the second millennium BC. At the beginning of that period, it has been maintained, speakers of an early form of what was to be known as Greek entered the north-western area, and while the majority of their descendants later moved on to Greece, some at least remained in Anatolia and were still in occupation of the north-west during the period of Hittite domination of central Anatolia. If this theory is acceptable, it has wide implications, for it not only raises the possibility of Hittite-Greek contacts in the area of the Troad; it also makes it possible to suggest that the Trojan War of Greek legend (traditionally dated to *c.* 1200 BC) was not a conflict between the alien worlds of Greece and Anatolia, but that, since the inhabitants of Troy at the time were in fact linguistically Greek, it was rather an inter-state conflict within the orbit of the Greek world of the time. This would certainly make it easier to understand why Troy plays such a large part in Greek tradition, and would suggest that the large number of personal contacts between Greeks and Trojans mentioned in the Homeric poems, and the ease with which opponents communicated with each other as they fought or parleyed, were something more than an elaborate poetic fiction.

In order to assess this theory it is necessary to turn for a moment to the possible origins of Greek. It has long been commonly accepted that the Greek language was introduced to Greece by newcomers who brought with them the type of pottery known as 'Minyan' ware. For many years the evidence available suggested that this pottery appeared in Greece about 1900 BC, at the beginning of the Middle Helladic period. Since very similar pottery was found at Troy, where it was 20 introduced at approximately the same date (early Troy VI), it seemed an obvious conclusion that there had been a two-pronged invasion from somewhere further north, with one group moving down into Greece and the other occupying north-western Anatolia. The inhabitants of Troy VI then, it could be assumed, spoke an early form of Greek. One difficulty in accepting this theory was that there were no signs at all of pottery ancestral to Minyan ware in the areas north of Greece and in the Balkans where it might have been expected to appear. A further

20 Greek and Anatolian 'Minyan' ware: *top*, from Korakou, Middle Helladic period; *above*, from Tavşanlı, Troy V period (after Mellaart).

complication was added when it was suggested that Trojan Minyan (and therefore presumably Greek Minyan as well) could be seen to have its ancestry in the latter part of the Early Bronze Age in the region south and east of the Sea of Marmara. The conclusion to be drawn from this was that proto-Greek speakers had entered Anatolia earlier in the Early Bronze Age, had stayed there for some time, and had then crossed by sea to central Greece at the beginning of the following period, leaving some of their number to develop the culture of Troy VI.[20]

More recent research, however, seems to indicate that both these theories are based on false premises. Minyan pottery has now been found in Greece, most notably at Lerna in the Argolid, in EH III contexts. This can be explained away by claiming that *some* proto-Greek speakers had crossed from Anatolia earlier than others. But this is contradicted by studies which suggest that the EH III culture as a whole is the result, not of immigration from Anatolia, but of a period of indigenous development in central Greece preceded by influences which came ultimately from the Baden culture of Austria-Hungary, a culture which in turn can be linked with the spread of *Kurgan* features into central Europe.[21] Further analysis of Anatolian 'Minyan' also suggests that the resemblances between it and Greek Minyan are largely illusory, and that the two have different origins and different developments.[22] So theories that there were Greeks in north-west Anatolia during the Middle and Late Bronze Ages seem to be without foundation. Yet a certain amount of doubt remains. Although detailed examination of the two types of pottery shows that shared shapes were almost non-existent, the overall similarity in appearance and in fabric can be felt to be too close to be accidental. And when in the first millennium the north-west emerges into written history, it is part of the Greek world, occupied by Greek-speaking peoples. But the arrival of these 'Aeolic' Greeks from Greece, unlike that of the Ionians further south, cannot yet be recognized without doubt in the archaeological record, for first-millennium pottery in the area seems to be directly descended from that of the second millennium, rather than introduced from any outside source. Nor can the scanty foundation legends of the Aeolic settlements inspire great confidence in their historical accuracy. Only further excavation and research can show whether the Aeolic Greeks were in fact immigrants from across the Aegean or the descendants of Greek-speaking natives of the second millennium, the 'Trojans' of the Homeric poems.

Luwians in Greece

Another theory which suggests close linguistic connections between Anatolia and Greece centres on the many place-names ending in -anthos, -assos, and similar forms, which are to be found on either side of the Aegean. These endings can plausibly be explained as Luwian, and their distribution suggests that Luwian, or rather its linguistic ancestor, was at some time spoken over large areas of both western Anatolia and Greece. It has been suggested that it was 'Luwians' (rather than Greeks) who arrived in Greece at the beginning of the Middle Helladic period (*c.* 1900 BC), or even that they arrived as late as the Shaft Grave period (*c.* 1600 BC). But, as was pointed out long ago, there is a remarkable coincidence between the distribution of place-names of this type and that of sites with Early Helladic II connections.[23] The origins of numerous features of the Aegean Early Bronze Age have been seen in western Anatolia. These may well be explicable in terms of trading contacts. But since, accepting the arguments presented above, western Anatolia was already at that time proto-Luwian in speech, there is something to be said for a contemporary linguistic spread to the Greek mainland. On this hypothesis Greek was not the first Indo-European language in Greece, but was preceded in the area by a 'proto-Luwian' linguistic element which was widespread during the earlier part of the Early Bronze Age.

Conclusions

Is there then an answer to the question posed in the title of this chapter? To some extent at least there is, but it must first be emphasized that we cannot define the Hittites, or any of their contemporaries, in terms of their physical appearance. There is nothing that can be labelled uniquely 'Hittite' in the shape of their skulls, or the colour of their skin, eyes or hair. In political and chronological terms definition is much easier. The Hittites, the Arzawans and other peoples who have been mentioned above occupied neighbouring areas of second-millennium Anatolia, and their history, and many aspects of their life, will be the subjects of subsequent chapters. But to limit our definition in this way is to ignore a very important part of what we know about the Hittites and their contemporaries – their languages. Using this as a tool we can define a Hittite as someone who used the Hittite language, an Arzawan   21, 22 as a speaker (or writer) of Luwian, the language of Arzawa, and so on. This opens up a much wider area of enquiry, for it can then be seen that much of second-millennium Anatolia was occupied by speakers of languages which were closely related to each other and which, more importantly, have their origins in the Indo-European family of which large numbers of modern languages, including our own, are also members. Linguistic evidence can to some extent be linked to the evidence of archaeology, and in this way we can hope to trace the history of the Hittites and Arzawans (i.e. speakers of Hittite and Luwian, or rather their immediate ancestor, perhaps better referred to as proto-Anatolic) back into earlier millennia, long before the existence of any written documentation of their existence. We can also recognize the possibility that speakers of a closely related language were to be found in third-millennium Greece and the Aegean, and there is at least something to be said for the theory that north-west Anatolia was occupied by speakers of an early form of Greek (also Indo-European, but belonging to a different branch of the family). In Hattian we have evidence for at least one of the languages spoken in central Anatolia before the arrival of the Indo-European-speakers. Thus in our search for the origins of the Hittites and their neighbours the evidence of language enables us to go back far beyond the boundaries imposed by any historical material contained in surviving texts.

3

The Hittites and their neighbours

In chapter 1 we saw how trade between Anatolia and Assyria was ended about 1780 BC when the routes along which merchandise travelled were cut by the increasingly active Hurrian states of northern Mesopotamia. We saw, too, how the kings of Kussara took advantage of this situation to gain control of much of central Anatolia. In fact the speedy removal of their capital westward to Kanesh/Nesas was probably a direct result of Hurrian pressure, for Kussara itself, if it lay near modern Divriği, was uncomfortably close to the newly emergent powers. Central Anatolia, however, provided its own problems, for there too there were unruly neighbours, and it was perhaps the presence of such neighbours, most notably the state of Zalpa, on the northern frontier, that led a prince of the royal house about 1650 BC to decide that strategic considerations were of greater importance than the curse of Anittas, and to build a new fortress at the long deserted but naturally defensible site of Hattusas. The Hurrian advance continued, and it may be supposed that when the eastern parts of the Kussaran realm fell to them Hattusilis – 'man of Hattusas', as the prince now styled himself – was left as an independent monarch, the founder of what we now call the Hittite Old Kingdom.

Hattusilis I

Hattusilis quickly set about consolidating and expanding his kingdom. The direction of his expansion may well have been based on economic considerations, for the loss of the Assyrian connection must also have meant the loss of essential tin-supplies, and an alternative source had to be found. The obvious alternative was, as we have seen, the route which ran up the Euphrates valley from Babylonia to the Mediterranean coastlands, and it was towards the control of this route that his policy, and that of his successors, was directed. The rough outlines of what happened can be reconstructed from surviving contemporary documents and later references.[24] From them it can be seen that Hattusilis's first action was the conquest of the cities that lay between his capital and the Cilician Gates. Once these cities were secured, he could move down into Cilicia and reach the Mediterranean Sea. Here, on the threshold of the Syro-Mesopotamian world, he could build fortresses like that at Mersin (originally ascribed by the excavators to a later period) and make preparations for his attack on the trade-route. The enemy against whom his efforts were directed was Aleppo, the power in command of the northern terminus of the route. But Aleppo was much too strong to be dealt with at one blow. First the Hittite king turned on Alalah, the principal port of the area, thus robbing Aleppo of its outlet to the sea. Fortunately for us, the site of Alalah has been excavated, and the Hittite attack may be convincingly equated with the destruction of Level VII of the site, an event which can be dated to between 1650 and 1600 BC.[25]

The geography of western Anatolia

After capturing Alalah, Hattusilis moved against Urshu, a little to the north, and other allies of Aleppo. But before he could complete the isolation of his enemy, he turned in a completely different direction. His opponent on this occasion was Arzawa, which we have already met as the principal power of western Anatolia. Unfortunately, written documents have yet to be recovered from this area, and what little is known of it comes from fairly meagre archaeological results and from references in the texts of other peoples, notably the Hittites and the Egyptians. As a result of this lack of evidence, the geography of western Anatolia in the second millennium BC has for long been a subject of considerable dispute. But since the reconstruction and interpretation of the history of the Hittites is dependent to a great extent on an assessment of the geographical positions of their neighbours, it is essential first to consider these in a little detail.

The state of Arzawa is the focal point of the area, and round it are grouped the 'Arzawa-countries' of Mira, Hapalla and the Seha River Land, closely attached to Arzawa itself by linguistic and dynastic ties. The main evidence for establishing the positions of these countries lies in Hittite texts describing royal campaigns against them. From these texts a pattern of inter-relationships of towns and areas can be established. In relating this pattern to the Anatolian landscape, one has to take note of the few routes along which armies might march in a generally westerly direction from the Hittite homeland. Two such routes are of particular importance. One, the more northerly, proceeds more or less due west and ends up in the central part of the Aegean coastlands. A branch-route from it turns off after crossing the River Sakarya and proceeds in a rather more northerly direction until it reaches the Sea of Marmara. The other, southerly, route passes south of the central Salt Lake, runs through the Turkish 'Lake District', and finishes in the south-west, either in Pamphylia or in Lycia. The more southerly route has much in its favour in establishing the location of Arzawa. Arzawan attacks on Hittite territory often seem to impinge on the lands south of the Salt Lake, and it would therefore seem reasonable to suppose that Hittite attacks on Arzawa should start from the same area. On this basis the Arzawa-countries are to be located in the south-west, and since Arzawa itself has a coastline, the coast in question must be that of either Pamphylia or Lycia.

This conclusion seems eminently reasonable, but there is one big problem. Survey-work in Lycia and Pamphylia has so far shown no sign at all of settled occupation during the Hittite period. It is easy enough to accept that *some* sites in an area may have been overlooked, or that all settlements there were built of stone which was reused and so has left little or no trace, or that they were mere collections of wooden shacks on the hillsides or among the trees. But it is difficult to believe that *all* surface traces of a country as powerful as Arzawa, a country which, as we shall see, could challenge the power of the Hittites and at least try to correspond on an equal footing with Egypt, have so far defied all efforts to locate them. It must be said of course that in recent years it has become increasingly clear that many pre-Classical sites in the west are so deeply buried under layers of sediment, the result of large-scale erosion of more upland areas, that they have left little or no surface indication of their existence. It may therefore be that all traces of even the largest settlements of Arzawa, if it lay in the south-west, have been obliterated in this way. But until such time as there *is* physical evidence for the existence of considerable sites of the appropriate period, the identification of Arzawa with south-western Anatolia remains a matter of grave doubt.

The alternative is to follow the other, more northerly, route, and see Arzawa as lying in the area of Classical Lydia, with its coast along the Aegean around Classical Ephesus and Smyrna. In either case the 'Arzawa-countries' have to be placed in some way between Arzawa and Hittite territory, since in texts dealing with military campaigns hostile action from Hittite lands seems to affect them before it reaches Arzawa itself.

22

21 Alternative map of Anatolia in Hittite times.

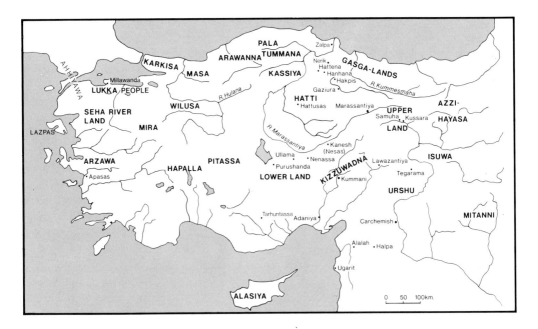

22 Map of Anatolia in Hittite times.

Other western lands must also be mentioned here. Wilusa was sometimes recognized as an Arzawa-country, but was for long periods closely allied to the Hittites. There has for many years been a strong temptation to link its name with (W)ilion and make it include the site of Ilion/Troy. But it is difficult to imagine that an extremely strong link with central Anatolia could have been preserved over many years if Wilusa lay in the remote and rather inaccessible Troad. A position closer to Hittite territory, perhaps in or near the Plain of Eskişehir, seems much more likely. Then there are the Lukka Lands. These too are clearly western; but they are elusive, and have been located in areas as far apart as Lycia, Lycaonia and the southern shores of the Sea of Marmara. The answer here, it has recently been pointed out, may well be that 'Lukka' is the Hittite for what in western terms is called Luwiya, and is a linguistic rather than a geographical term – that is, it means 'Luwian-speaking' rather than 'living in a Lukka Land'.[26] This may in the end help to explain how Lukka-people keep popping up in unexpected places, and may save us from having to postulate two or more Lukka Lands, or large-scale migrations of Lukka-people for unknown reasons from one area to another completely different one.

Ahhiyawa

This leaves Millawanda and Ahhiyawa, and brings us to the most controversial question of all. Ever since Forrer's proposal in 1924 that the Ahhiyawans of the Hittite texts were to be equated with the Homeric Achaeans, and consequently with the Mycenaean Greeks, academic opinion has been sharply divided between support and rejection of his view. Philhellenic scholars claim that Hittites and Mycenaeans cannot fail to have made contact in the Aegean and eastern

Mediterranean, that the contact, when it is made, is at just the times, and at just the places, where one might expect it, and that the resemblance of names between the Achaeans and the Ahhiyawans is more than fortuitous. Anti-Mycenaeans allege that archaeologically there is little evidence for contact, that there is nothing in the texts to suggest that Ahhiyawa is outside Anatolia, and that the equation of the names is a philological impossibility.

In a conflict of this nature one has to take sides, and the author must admit at once that although he would like to accept the equation with Mycenaeans, he still feels that the balance of evidence is against it. This view is based mainly on the wider question of Anatolian geography, for Ahhiyawa and Millawanda, a coastal city under Ahhiyawan influence, are closely linked with areas such as the Seha River Land, which are, if one accepts that Arzawa occupied the central Aegean coast, and that the south-west was virtually unoccupied, to be located in the north-western corner of Anatolia. The Mycenaean theory is largely based on the equation of Millawanda with Miletus, where there is a known Mycenaean settlement. Attractive though this equation is, it creates several problems which will have to be resolved before it can gain universal acceptance.

It is for instance hard to see how Millawanda, if it is Miletus, can be fitted into the pattern of western Anatolian states without placing some of them, including Arzawa, in the problematical south-western area; and even if one can interpret the geographical evidence in a way which keeps Arzawa in Lydia, it is equally difficult to see how relations between the Hittites and Millawanda/Ahhiyawa, whether friendly or otherwise, could have been maintained at times when a hostile Arzawa lay between the two. It is also necessary to assume from the textual evidence that Mycenaean raiders were already penetrating well up onto the Anatolian plateau as early as 1450, and for this there is no visible evidence – although it can of course be reasonably claimed that such raiding parties would be unlikely to leave any recognizable physical trace of their presence.[27] Then there is the evidence of a treaty drawn up about 1230 between the Hittites and the land of Amurru on the Levantine coast. In this treaty the ruler of Amurru is forbidden to allow ships of Ahhiyawa to trade through the ports of Amurru with Assyria, at that time a Hittite enemy. Now it is true that there is abundant evidence of Mycenaean trade in the Levant, and evidence too of that trade greatly declining c. 1250–30.[28] But it is important to remember that Mycenaean trade was purely coastal in character. There is no evidence at all of Mycenaean goods penetrating far inland and passing through Levantine territory to be received in Assyria. If the trade was of sufficient importance for a Hittite king to try to put a stop to it, one might expect some signs of Mycenaean pottery east of the Euphrates.

Nevertheless the Ahhiyawa/Mycenaean Greek equation has over the years been strongly and persuasively argued,[29] and it is with some hesitation that the alternative view is maintained here. It has in the end to be admitted that the evidence is at present insufficient to offer conclusive proof for either case. What we really need before we can accept one side or the other is something rather more secure than deductions made from the Homeric poems on what, if anything, the Mycenaeans called themselves. Evidence from Linear B texts would be invaluable, as would information from some outside source – say Ugarit – on what Mycenaeans were called by their contemporaries.[30] One day such evidence may be found; but that day is not yet. Until it comes, one has to take up the position which seems to one to be the most probable in terms of the evidence there is. Accordingly, the historical reconstruction which follows in this book is based on the assumption that Millawanda lay on the shores of the Sea of Marmara,   22 and that Ahhiyawa too was situated, at least in part, in north-west Anatolia, and very probably included territory on the European shores of the Sea of Marmara as well.[31] However, an alternative map is provided, with Millawanda at Miletus and Arzawa in the south-west,   21 and those who disagree with the reconstruction can follow their own geographical pattern and reinterpret the narrative accordingly. But the author feels a certain amount of justification in claiming that if the arrangement of states suggested above is accepted, the overall picture of Anatolian geography and history makes sense. Events fit into a general pattern of economic necessity, and the efforts of the various states can be seen to be directed towards something more permanent than the arbitrary ambitions of individual sovereigns.

The problem of tin supplies

In attempting to justify this view we may now return to Hattusilis and his campaign against Arzawa. Its purpose is unknown. He may have been attacked from behind when his attention was directed to the south-east, but equally his expedition may be linked with one ascribed to 'Labarnas' in a later treaty, in the course of which both Arzawa and Wilusa were conquered. If we now ask what the importance of Wilusa was, a glance at the map will show us, for Wilusa lay astride the branch   22 of the northern route, previously mentioned, which led from the Land of Hatti to north-western Anatolia and from there across the straits into Europe. Was it then trade which provoked Hittite interest in this route, as had economic factors in the south-east also? And if so, what articles or materials came to Hattusas along the route? We can only guess, for no Hittite monarch ever gives any hint of economic motives in attacking, making a treaty with, or otherwise seeking to influence another country.

It has been suggested that this route too was a tin-route,[32] leading through the Balkans and eventually to the rich resources of Bohemia. And that leads us directly to the vexed question of the source, or sources, of the tin which was widely used in the manufacture of bronze in ancient Anatolia. In considering this question, already touched on in chapter 1, one must take into account evidence from the Early and Middle Bronze Ages as well as the Hittite period. It is clear for instance that in the third millennium BC the percentage of copper-based artifacts containing more than five per cent tin is much higher in north-western and central Anatolia (and also north-western Iran) than it is in neighbouring areas such as Mesopotamia, Syria, Egypt and Crete. The obvious conclusion to be drawn from this is that there was a tin-source somewhere in (central?) Anatolia which was available to local metal-workers. But herein lies the core of the problem, for despite the most intense investigation no such tin-source has yet been found. The problem becomes more acute when we move into the second millennium, for not only Anatolia, but neighbouring areas as well, can be seen to have access to supplies of tin for bronze-making, and still there is no clear indication of any source within the area from which it could have come. We have, it seems, to accept the fact that the tin which was used in the Mediterranean basin, Anatolia, western Iran and Mesopotamia, came from somewhere outside those areas, and that trade in tin played a considerable part in economic life.

But where did the tin come from? One possible source is the eastern desert of Egypt, the only area within easy reach of the Mediterranean and Mesopotamian worlds where there are known sources of cassiterite (stannic dioxide, $Sn O_2$), the form in which tin was most easily available to ancient prospectors. But there is no evidence either for the third-millennium exploitation of this tin or for the second-millennium use of Egyptian tin as a trade-item, and we regretfully have to look elsewhere. If we turn first of all to the east we find, as we have seen, tin being imported to central Anatolia from Assyria. But the source of that tin has for long been obscure. Such evidence as there is points to somewhere beyond the Zagros Mountains. Until recently, however, no possible source had been identified between the Iranian border and India. So it was suggested that tin came to Mesopotamia from as far afield as Thailand and Malaysia, being imported by sea up the Arabian Gulf. But there is certainly no evidence for trading-connections between Thailand and the Gulf, and it is very difficult to see the tin used in Anatolia (which is our main concern here) as having its ultimate origin as far away as south-east Asia. However in recent years a new possibility has emerged with the discovery of major tin deposits in Afghanistan.[33] It may then be that Afghan tin was brought overland to Assur, and it is also possible that it was carried south from Afghanistan to the coast and then brought by ship up the Arabian Gulf to Mesopotamian ports, where it was loaded on to donkeys for transport up-river to the north, and distribution *via* the Assyrian trade-network in Anatolia.

A solution such as this may help to explain the early second-millennium import of tin into central Anatolia from the south-east. But it offers no help in explaining why the percentage of tin-bronzes in third-millennium Anatolia – and especially in the north-west – is much higher than that in Mesopotamia. This evidence suggests that there must have been another tin-source, and the likelihood is that it was somewhere west, rather than east, of Anatolia. So if we turn now to the west, we have to ask ourselves whether importation of British tin from the prolific mines of Cornwall is a possibility. There seems to be a complete lack of tin-bronze in Britain itself before about 2200 BC, and this makes it totally unlikely that Cornwall was the source of the tin used in Anatolian bronzes in the third millennium. After 2200, however, objects of tin-bronze in Britain increase greatly in numbers, and the export of objects made of British tin-bronze into northern and central Europe has been noted. This export-trade may have been associated with the export of tin for use by continental smiths, and thus British tin may by the second millennium have been reaching the Mediterranean coast, whence it could have been carried by sea to ports on the shores of Anatolia. This is at least a possibility which has to be kept in mind, but it must be admitted that there is at present little or no evidence for it.

What of other possible sources? One such that cannot be left out of consideration is central Europe. Here, in the region of Bohemia, there are ample supplies of tin-ore, but as usual there are problems connected with it. The main one is that Bohemian tin occurs in the form of vein-deposits in granite rock, and because of the hardness of this rock it has been claimed that such deposits were completely inaccessible to ancient miners. This is largely true. But even the hardest rock yields in time to natural erosion, and because of this tin-ores may well have been available in quantities sufficient to make exploitation worth while. In fact the importation of tin from Britain, mentioned in the previous paragraph, may well have inspired central European prospectors to look more closely for local supplies. If these were available, an easy export-route led down the Danube valley to the Balkans, and so across the straits into north-western Turkey. Certainly central Europe had trade-connections as far afield as Syria not long after the beginning of the second millennium,[34] and towards the end of that millennium a trail of objects with spiral decoration has been taken to show that the Mycenaeans also used the route. But these decorations could equally well have originated in north-west Anatolia, and there is no trace of pottery or anything else that can be unequivocally ascribed to the Mycenaeans.[35] It is therefore possible to argue that supplies of central European tin (or even Cornish tin passing through central Europe) reached Anatolia by way of this north-western route. Admittedly the arguments in its favour are weak; but so too are the arguments for any alternative source. It is little wonder that increasingly those who study the problem are turning once more to a native Anatolian tin-source, undetected and, because totally exhausted, probably undetectable.[36] But faced with a choice between an invisible local source and a variety of equally improbable outside sources, the author feels once again that he has to make a decision. And since the geographical reconstruction proposed above, however insubstantial its basis, points clearly to a continuing Hittite involvement with the north-west, he feels it worth while to accept as a working hypothesis the theory of a central European tin-source, and to interpret Hittite history and Hittite policy accordingly.

Western Anatolia is of course no richer in tin-deposits than central Anatolia, and we may also be justified in seeing in Bohemia the ultimate source of the tin that was needed by the kings of Arzawa. It is then a reasonable guess that in conquering Arzawa and forging a link with Wilusa that was to last almost unbroken for hundreds of years, Hattusilis (we return at last to our starting-point) had the same motive as we have ascribed to him when he attacked Alalah and the south-eastern route. In each case the object of his campaign may well have been tin.

Old Kingdom campaigns

A Hurrian counter-attack soon forced Hattusilis to turn eastwards again. The whole of the Land of Hatti, except its capital, fell into their hands, but within a year or two the Hittite king had driven them back through the Taurus passes, and was able to advance to the Euphrates. About this time too the ancient capital of Kussara must have been recaptured, and we also hear of successes on the north-eastern frontier. In this area too metal-supplies may have been the ultimate motive for the king's interest. Despite these successes, however, Hattusilis was unable to defeat his first opponent, Aleppo, and he may have received a mortal wound while trying to do so.

His death left the final conquest of north Syria to Mursilis, his grandson and successor. It occurred to this monarch that diplomacy might bring success where force had failed, so he applied himself to the problem of disrupting the trade-route to his own advantage. Aleppo at its northern end was still much too strong to succumb to Hittite pressure. Babylon at its southern end was weak, but allied to Aleppo. On the middle Euphrates, however, Mari had now disappeared and the new power in the area was the kingdom of Hana. This state was not under Amorite rule like Babylon and Aleppo, but had recently come under the influence of the Kassites, a foreign people from the Iranian hills. The obvious course was an alliance with Hana to encircle Aleppo, disrupt her trade and reduce her prosperity, and it is probable that this move was made. We have few details of what happened, but about 1595 Mursilis descended from Anatolia and succeeded in destroying Aleppo.

Thus the south-eastern trade-route came under Hittite control at least as far as the middle Euphrates. Mursilis had gained what he needed, but his allies in Hana were not satisfied, and persuaded him that greater glory was at hand. Thus spurred on, Mursilis swept down the Euphrates and descended on Babylon. The dynasty of Hammurabi was brought to a humiliating end, and the Hittites arrived in force on the international field.

The conquest of Babylon cannot have been more than a rash venture by the Hittite king. Physical control of the entire trade-route was not necessary for his purpose and he soon returned to his homeland, leaving the images of the deities of Babylon, and doubtless a part of its treasure, with his allies at Hana. Continuing Hurrian pressure would have made it difficult to hold on to such distant conquests, and palace rivalries in Hattusas also helped in persuading him to withdraw. Shortly afterwards Mursilis was murdered by his brother-in-law, and with his death the Hittite conquests began to crumble away. Under his successors the Hurrians, now led by a dynasty with Indo-Aryan connections, advanced again through north Syria and into Cilicia, the peoples of the northern hills captured the holy city of Nerik and forced the refortification of Hattusas itself, and Arzawa broke away and regained its independence. By the time of the accession of Telepinus (c. 1500) the kingdom was confined once again to central Anatolia. Telepinus however was able to consolidate his position sufficiently to advance once more in the direction of north Syria, win several victories in the Anti-Taurus area, and conclude an alliance with the ruler of

22

Kizzuwadna, a new power which had been established in Cilicia by a Hurrian or Indo-Aryan dynasty.

From Middle Kingdom to Empire

With Telepinus what is usually known as the Old Kingdom comes to an end. Its achievements had been ephemeral, but the policies of its kings set a pattern which was to be followed in all its essentials by the monarchs of the later and greater Hittite Empire. This is the name normally given to the period between about 1450 and 1180 BC. Its history has recently been complicated by the fact that a number of documents, previously assigned to the reign of Tudhaliyas IV towards the end of the period, can now plausibly be taken to describe events in the reign of a much earlier Tudhaliyas, probably the first king of that name, who reigned at the beginning of the Empire.[37] The obscure period between the Old Kingdom and the Empire, sometimes known as the Middle Kingdom, is one of almost unrelieved Hittite decline. Only a treaty with a king of Kizzuwadna shows a temporary success against the Hurrians, now organized and unified as the north Mesopotamian kingdom of Mitanni and eager to gain control of the Euphrates route. At this time too the attraction of northern Syria, with its rich trade and wealth of natural products, brought another major power on to the scene in the shape of Egypt. Shortly after 1440 Tuthmosis III advanced up the Levantine coast and conquered Aleppo.

These new developments were highly unwelcome to the Hittites, but they prudently paid tribute to Egypt and waited for their opportunity. It came when Aleppo rebelled against Egypt on the death of Tuthmosis *c.* 1436, but although this rebellion may have been instigated by the Hittites, Aleppo was sufficiently ungrateful to transfer her allegiance to Mitanni. This was the situation when Tudhaliyas I came to the throne shortly after, and his action was swift and decisive. First the alliance with Kizzuwadna was renewed, and within a year or two of his accession he was able to meet and defeat both Aleppo and Mitanni. The south-eastern trade-route was once again in Hittite hands.

Tudhaliyas than turned to the west, and campaigns followed against Arzawa and the Seha River Land. To the north-west, a number of smaller states on or near the route to Europe had banded together to form a confederation under the general name of Assuwa. As this name does not appear in any later document, it must be assumed that after its defeat Assuwa broke up again into its constituent parts. At this time too 21 Ahhiyawa first appears in the Hittite records as a hostile power whose king Attarsiyas at least twice attacked the Hittite vassal Madduwattas. But despite temporary successes in this direction it is clear that Tudhaliyas failed to achieve lasting control of the north-western route.

To the north of the Hittite realms there was trouble in the Gasga-lands, which were from then on to be constantly hostile to the Hittites. This may indeed have been the very time at which the Gasga-people were moving into the northern coastlands. Further east the Hurrians were making up for their lack of success in north Syria by wooing the kings of the Armenian mountains. It is probable that Tudhaliyas

22 directed a campaign against the north-eastern country known both as Azzi and as Hayasa, and he certainly had to deal with Isuwa, a land which lay across the Euphrates around modern Elazığ. Little is known of this campaign, but it may be pointed out that on the borders of Isuwa are to be found the most important copper-mines in the Middle East (the modern Erganı Maden). These had been known to the Assyrian merchants centuries earlier, and their presence in the border-area between Hatti and Mitanni must surely be regarded as an important factor in the enmity of these powers.

The reign of Tudhaliyas was followed by another period of disaster. North Syria and Kizzuwadna were rapidly lost, and enemies from all sides – the Gasga-lands to the north, Azzi-Hayasa to the north-east, Isuwa to the east, and several other countires besides – closed in on Hattusas and burnt it to the ground. The Land of Hatti was so weakened by these attacks that the king of Arzawa was able to ignore it while he struck across the southern Anatolian plateau towards the approaches to the Cilician Gates. Clearly he too was interested in the south-eastern trade-route, and had ambitions to succeed the Hittite king as an international figure. This can be seen also in the Arzawa letter from el Amarna (mentioned in chapter 2) in which there was talk of a marriage-connection with the Egyptian royal house. Nothing tells us that any marriage took place, but the fact that it was suggested shows that the Arzawan monarch sought to be regarded as the equal of the other Great Kings of the Middle Eastern world.

Suppiluliumas I

The triumph of Arzawa did not last. About 1380 the Hittite throne was seized by an energetic young prince called Suppiluliumas, a man who had already before his accession shown by victories in the north-east, north and north-west that he could deal with his country's enemies. An early attack on Mitanni was a failure, although it may have resulted in the temporary recovery of Isuwa. Later, Isuwa was recaptured on a more permanent basis, and Kizzuwadna and the 'Hurri-land', a powerful north Syrian rival of Mitanni, were linked by treaty to the Land of Hatti. Thus Suppiluliumas was in a much stronger position when he moved again against Mitanni, and he very soon gained possession of the lands west of the Euphrates. Aleppo and other north Syrian states were conquered, and the Hittites were once more firmly established at the head of the Euphrates-route.

Suppiluliumas did not repeat his predecessor's mistake by venturing down river to Babylon. Instead he tactfully gained his objective by contracting a marriage with the Babylonian king's daughter. Then a Mitannian counter-attack towards Isuwa was made the pretext for a strong Hittite campaign which succeeded in capturing the Mitannian capital and destroying its remaining power. Finally an attack was mounted on Carchemish, a powerful state situated at the point where the Euphrates comes nearest to the Mediterranean coast, and with its fall Suppiluliumas was able to organize north Syria on a basis which would ensure continuing Hittite supremacy. Carchemish and Aleppo were made into vassal-states under the rule of two of the king's sons, and further east potential danger from Assyria, which had gained its independence at the fall of Mitanni, was counterbalanced by the creation of a new Mitanni subject to the Hittites and acting as a buffer-state against danger from its former subject. Even Egypt almost became a sphere of Hittite influence when the widow of Tutankhamun wrote to Suppiluliumas asking for one of his sons to be her husband. Unfortunately for the Hittite king his son was murdered on the way to Egypt and the proposed alliance did not take place.

In the west Suppiluliumas did not meet with such great success. He had already defeated the army of Arzawa before he came to the throne, and shortly after his accession he drove it back across the Konya Plain from the approaches to the Cilician Gates as far as Mira and Hapalla. But it is unlikely that the land of Arzawa itself was conquered, and it remained a constant danger to the south-western parts of the Hittite realms.

To the north-west the situation was rather different. Dependent as he must have been on supplies of tin to equip his forces in Syria, Suppiluliumas made every effort to keep this trade-route open. The Seha River Land was on the whole an effective buffer against aggression from Arzawa, and Ahhiyawa was now a friendly power, probably bound by treaty to the Hittites. The only danger came towards the end of the Hittite king's reign when Millawanda was persuaded by Arzawa to rebel and seek Ahhiyawan assistance. Mira and the Seha River Land were also involved, and the situation must have been rather ugly. Suppiluliumas however was too deeply involved in north Syria to attend to things himself, and the solution of this problem was left to his son Mursilis.

In the north-east Suppiluliumas succeeded in making an alliance with the king of Azzi-Hayasa, but the northern Gasga-people were a constant source of trouble, and yearly campaigns were necessary to cope with their unending raids.

Mursilis II

Suppiluliumas died about 1334 of a plague which his soldiers had brought back from a Syrian campaign. His eldest son quickly followed him to the grave, and the throne passed to his younger son Mursilis, who proved to be an effective successor to his father. Fortunately for him, there was no need for immediate action to defend the south-eastern route. The buffer-state of Mitanni, backed by the armed forces of Carchemish, was able for a time to absorb the aggressive energies of Assyria, and Egypt was still recovering from a period of weakness and was as yet unwilling to extend her influence into north Syria. Thus Mursilis was able to attend to the north-western route. Millawanda, which had caused trouble at the end of his father's reign, was quickly defeated. Then Mursilis mounted a full-scale and highly successful attack on the Arzawa lands. On its conclusion Arzawa itself was awarded to a presumably pro-Hittite member of its royal family,[38] while Mira, Hapalla and the Seha River Land were created separate vassal-states, bound by elaborate treaties to the Land of Hatti. Thus Arzawa was encircled by a line of states which separated her both from   22

47

23–4 Impressions of royal seals. *Top*: Muwatallis (see p. 102); *above*: Mursilis III (Urhi-Teshub).

the Land of Hatti and from the tin-route. Clearly Mursilis hoped that he would have no more trouble in the west, and for the remainder of his lifetime and throughout that of his successor his policy proved remarkably effective.

In other directions Mursilis met with similar success. The Gasga-people continued their attacks from the north, and finally Mursilis established a firm line of border-fortresses under military control which did succeed in containing his enemies, if not in conquering them. Further east Azzi-Hayasa rebelled but was defeated again, and in Syria Mitanni, which had eventually fallen to the Assyrians, was probably recaptured. All over the empire the emphasis was on good organization and firm control through vassal-states, a policy which became increasingly necessary with the revival of Egypt and the renewal of her interest in northern Syria. The latter part of Mursilis's reign was certainly directed towards preparation for the inevitable clash of powers, and there is no record of any further expansionist policy at this time. In the far north-west there was a certain amount of trouble from Piyamaradus of Millawanda, an unruly vassal who had transferred his allegiance to Ahhiyawa.[39] Mursilis, preoccupied by the growing danger from Egypt, was content to lead an expedition to Millawanda and ask for the extradition of Piyamaradus, who had fled to an area under Ahhiyawan control. His request was probably granted, and it is likely that Piyamaradus gave a promise of good conduct and was restored to his throne.

Muwatallis

The reign of Muwatallis (*c.* 1308–1285) is rather poorly documented, as the destruction of Hattusas by the Gasga-people and the growing danger from Egypt caused him to move his capital from Hattusas to a more southerly site, perhaps near modern Karaman,[40] and the full records of his reign have yet to be discovered. The growing menace from the south also made it even more vitally important that there should be no trouble in the west. Yet Arzawa was restive, and in the north-west Piyamaradus was misbehaving again. So a quick western campaign was necessary, and although no details are known, it was clearly a success. The loyalty of the vassal-states was assured, and the Seha River Land, the vital buffer between Arzawa and the tin-route, was bound even more closely to the Hittite realms. The result was that when the Egyptian attack finally came, large contingents from the western states served in the Hittite army. But Hittite control must have been rather precarious, for it can be seen that Muwatallis regarded the west as a source of potential rebellion. Clearly disaffection was liable to break out at any moment.

Along the northern border skirmishing with the Gasga-people continued, but with one disastrous exception the fortified line established by Mursilis held, and this meant that the northerners could be kept in check by a comparatively small number of troops. Thus almost all the forces of the Hittite Empire could be concentrated where they were most needed, in north Syria, to meet the advance of the Egyptian pharaoh Rameses II. When the two armies met, at Qadesh on the River Orontes in *c.* 1286, the result was a victory for the Hittites, and their control of northern Syria remained unimpaired.[41] Yet the war had very serious consequences for Muwatallis, for while his efforts were concentrated on stopping Egypt, Assyria took advantage of the situation to defeat Mitanni and make it an Assyrian vassal.

25

Hattusilis III

Thus despite the glorious victory of Qadesh, the Hittite Empire was in considerable danger from both east and west. When Muwatallis died about 1285 the situation rapidly worsened, for throughout his short reign his son Urhi-Teshub, who succeeded as Mursilis III, was preoccupied by a quarrel with his uncle Hattusilis, whom he rightly suspected of having designs on the throne. On this issue the lands of western Anatolia were sharply divided. The Seha River Land was strongly in favour of Hattusilis, while Mira and possibly Ahhiyawa supported Mursilis. The course of events is obscure, but it is clear that after the deposition and exile of Mursilis by Hattusilis (*c.* 1278) most of the western lands disappear from the Hittite records. Hattusilis boasts that all those who were well-disposed to his predecessors were equally well-disposed to him, but there is little or no evidence to substantiate this claim for western Anatolia. One has to assume that the Arzawa-lands took advantage of the situation to shake off Hittite control.[42] Only in the north-west, along the vital tin-route, did the Hittites make any

25 Rameses II at Qadesh. Detail from a relief at the Ramesseum, Egyptian Thebes.

effort to retain an interest. Fighting in the Lukka Lands is mentioned in the fragmentary annals of Hattusilis, and the Seha River Land remained a Hittite dependency. Millawanda may have been a Hittite vassal again, and gifts were still exchanged between Hatti and Ahhiyawa.

The situation in Syria was almost as serious. Egypt had been defeated, but Adadnirari I of Assyria had taken advantage of a revolt in Mitanni to incorporate all the territory as far as the Euphrates into his realm. The south-eastern route was thus in great danger. A hasty and transitory alliance was arranged with Babylon, and finally the mutual danger brought Hattusilis and Rameses together. Their treaty stressed the reality of Hittite control over northern Syria, and the Egyptian renunciation of claims to that area, but clearly the agreement was largely meaningless. While the Hittite king was engaged in making arrangements for his daughter to marry Rameses, or for a summit meeting somewhere in Palestine, the Assyrians were consolidating their position further east and moving up into the hills which bordered on Anatolia. The climax to this movement came when the Assyrian king Shalmaneser I reached the Euphrates near Malatya. In the course of this campaign he must have succeeded in finally wresting from Hittite hands the control of the copper-mines of Isuwa.

26 Hattusilis III brings his daughter to be married to Rameses II. From an Egyptian relief at Abu Simbel (after Pritchard).

Tudhaliyas IV

The loss of his richest metal-source was a serious blow to the Hittite king, although it was partially offset by the fact that further south, around Carchemish, Hittite forces had succeeded in containing the Assyrian advance. This meant that the ports of the Syrian coast were still in Hittite hands, and it was probably with the help of a Syrian fleet that Tudhaliyas IV (c. 1250–1220), the son and successor of Hattusilis, invaded Cyprus, where he could find ample supplies of copper safe from Assyrian attack. To make this doubly certain, a Hittite treaty with Amurru, on the Syrian coast, included a clause prohibiting commercial relations of any kind between Amurru and Assyria.

Thus along the south-eastern trade-route the position remained temporarily favourable to the Hittites. In the north-west similar pressures were building up. Trouble in the Seha River Land was probably caused by Millawanda and backed by Ahhiyawa, and although Tudhaliyas was successful in gaining a victory, it is clear that his control of the area was slipping. Ahhiyawa was growing stronger, and could now be regarded – though temporarily or mistakenly – as one of the great powers of the Middle Eastern world. Arzawa too must have had an important part to play, but its relations with the other states of Anatolia, and with the Mycenaean Greeks along the Aegean coast, must await future discoveries for their clarification. It is clear, however, that the end of the Hittite Empire was at hand.

27 An ox-cart loaded with 'Sea People' under attack by the Egyptians. From an Egyptian relief at Medinet Habu (after Yadin).

The fall of the Hittite Empire

The successors of Tudhaliyas could do little to restore the situation. Harvests were failing, and grain had to be imported from as far afield as

Egypt to ward off famine. To the east, Assyrian pressure continued. In Syria the vassal-states were becoming lax in fulfilling their obligations, to the north the Gasga-people were an ever-present menace, and to the north-west there is an ominous silence. A temporary revival took place under a second Suppiluliumas (c. 1200–1180) who won the support of the Syrian vassals once more, defeated an enemy fleet, manned perhaps by rebellious vassals, perhaps by outside invaders, in a sea-battle off Cyprus, and even led a campaign into upper Mesopotamia in which he may have inflicted a defeat on the Assyrians and regained control of the Isuwan copper-mines. But all this was in vain. When the final blow came, it was not Assyria which delivered it. Far to the north-west a great migration was beginning which was to be stopped only on the borders of Egypt.[43] The reasons for this movement and the identity of the peoples who took part in it have been much discussed without any certain conclusions being reached, but it is evident that by the time the invasions reached Egypt (c. 1186) both Aegean and Anatolian peoples were involved in it. Yet whatever elements may have made up the invading force, its effect on Anatolia is clear. The north-western trade-route was the first to be cut. Arzawa, the great rival of the Hittites for its use, could not take advantage of the situation, for she too was swept away as the invaders moved down the Aegean coast and on along the Mediterranean shore. Cilicia fell to them, then Cyprus, and the great copper-source had gone. Finally the invaders reached and ravaged north Syria, causing the Hittites' second life-line to be severed. What happened afterwards at Hattusas is by no means clear. Certainly no Aegean seafarers came sailing up the Halys, but the centre of the

28 The final defeat of the 'Sea Peoples' by the Egyptians. Detail from a relief at Medinet Habu, Egyptian Thebes.

27, 28

empire was so weakened by the loss of the trade-routes that it could no longer resist the attacks of the ever-present Gasga-people and their neighbours to the north and east. The Land of Hatti was destroyed, and its capital was burnt to the ground.

So the Hittite Empire disappeared and was quickly forgotten. For two hundred and fifty years it had maintained its place as a leading power in the Middle Eastern world by a policy of keeping control of the routes by which vital raw materials reached it. This policy had been devised by the monarchs of the Old Kingdom, and its full implementation during the Imperial period gave the Hittites a position of strength and authority from which no other Middle Eastern state could dislodge them. Only when a completely new element was introduced and the trade-routes were cut by barbarian invasions from the north-west did this policy finally fail, and its failure, as Professor Goetze has said,[44] marked the end of an epoch.

Some misconceptions

Perhaps this is a suitable point at which to mention several mistaken ideas of the nature of Hittite power. The first of these is that the Hittites owed their dominant position to their monopoly of the production of a secret weapon called iron. For this there is, as far as I know, no evidence at all.[45] Secondly, it has been suggested that the superiority of the Hittites was due to the fact that they were ruled by an Indo-European aristocracy. The myth of Indo-European super-intelligence has been exploded long ago, but it is perhaps worth while to point out again that by the time of the foundation of the Hittite Old Kingdom (c. 1650) the invasion by speakers of an Indo-European language was already an event of the distant past, and that there is little or no evidence to suggest that the class-structure of the Hittite realm was based on considerations either of language or of race. The Hittites, like other peoples before and after them, were thoroughly hybrid in their racial make-up. Finally, the Hittites have been pictured as a horde of barbarous mountaineers who in 1595 flooded out from behind their barriers and descended, open-mouthed with greed and wonder, upon the ancient civilizations of Mesopotamia. I hope I have shown that Anatolia before the Hittite descent on Babylon was by no means as barbarous as this theory would have us think. On the contrary its traditions were as ancient, and its standards as high, as those of most parts of the contemporary Middle East. I have also tried to show that Hittite interest in Mesopotamia was based on economic principles which were rather more rational than simple barbarous greed.

Warfare and defence

North and north-east

The military and diplomatic problems which the Hittites faced in maintaining themselves were caused primarily by their geographical position and their economic needs. In order to understand these problems more fully it is necessary to look in some detail at the land of Hatti and its relations with neighbouring countries. Our starting-point may well be the city of Hattusas itself, and its situation on a rocky ridge looking north across a fertile plain turns our attention immediately in that direction. This rich agricultural land supplied much of the capital's corn, and its defence against the Gasga from the northern hills was a perpetual problem for the Hittite authorities. No permanent Gasgan conquest of the area was necessary; a yearly destruction of the crops was sufficient to disrupt the life of the capital. To prevent these annual raids some sort of frontier-line had to be established and maintained, and this was a constant preoccupation of Hittite kings throughout the period of the Empire. The strategic centre of this area was Hakpis (probably present-day Amasya), and from this town a line of fortified posts extended through such places as Hanhana and Hattena (perhaps near Merzifon and Gumushacıköy)[46] in the direction of the holy city of Nerik, situated possibly at Havza, or perhaps rather further north at Oymaağaç Tepe, north-west of Vezirköprü.[47] Nerik itself was dangerously close to Gasgan territory, and was for a long period in Gasgan hands. The strength of the northern frontier depended on constant patrolling between the fortified positions, and on the use of local inhabitants to spy and report on Gasgan movements. If the line broke, a last-ditch defence along a line running from Amasya through Çorum was possible. If this too fell, there was nothing to prevent a Gasgan descent on the capital itself.

Immediately east of Hakpis the frontier ran, probably through the narrow gorge of the Yeşil Irmak, to Gaziura at present-day Turhal. From there it continued until it reached the upper Halys somewhere between Sivas and Zara. Along this line too there was constant raiding by Gasga tribesmen, and although Hittite forces penetrated as far as the river Kummesmaha (possibly the Kelkit Çay) they were unable to gain any permanent advantage. Gasgan armies were able not only to devastate the area north of the Halys, but on occasion to cross the river and sweep down its southern bank towards Kanesh, near modern Kayseri, thus endangering the Hittites' most important communication-route with the east.

35, 68, 70

22

2

Somewhere in the hills east of Zara the Gasga-lands ended and the land of Azzi-Hayasa began. This country must have controlled the rich metal-deposits of north-eastern Anatolia, and although Suppiluliumas attempted to win access to these by diplomacy and Mursilis tried to gain the same end by force, there is little indication that the Hittites achieved any permanent footing in this area. They were able only to hold a frontier-line from the upper Halys to the Euphrates. Behind this line lay the buffer-province known as the Upper Land, with its administrative and religious centre at Samuha. This town has been placed by some scholars on the Halys, and by others on the Euphrates.[48] It may, in the author's opinion, have been situated at or near present-day Divriği. Strategically the Upper Land was extremely important, for if it fell it exposed to enemy attack the road from Sivas (perhaps Hittite Marassantiya) to the plain of Malatya (perhaps Hittite Tegarama), a road which was always an important Hittite route to northern Syria, and which indeed from the days of Mursilis I until the time of Suppiluliumas provided their only means of communication with that area.

22, 2 *(margin reference, opposite "near present-day Divriği")*

East and south-east

Across the Euphrates from the Malatya plain was the land of Isuwa, within whose boundaries lay the Ergani Maden, the richest copper-source in the Middle East. Its situation between Hatti and Mitanni made it a constant source of contention between these powers, and again it was Suppiluliumas who secured the area in Hittite hands. From then until its loss to Assyria in the reign of Hattusilis III (c. 1260 BC) the resources of Isuwa were available for the equipping of Hittite armies. Rescue excavations conducted at sites such as Norşuntepe, Korucutepe and Tepecik before their flooding by the waters of the Keban Dam scheme have provided clear evidence of strong Hittite influence on the area.

2 *(margin reference, opposite "within whose boundaries")*

The importance of the routes which lead from central Anatolia to northern Syria has already been sufficiently stressed. Apart from the Sivas-Malatya road, mentioned above, the principal routes were those which led from Kanesh (near modern Kayseri) through the passes of the Anti-Taurus mountains, the famous 'Cilician Gates' opening on to the plain of Cilicia, and the route which led down from the southern plateau at modern Karaman to the Mediterranean coast at Silifke and thence along the coast via Mersin, Tarsus and Adana. In the days before the rise of Hittite power Assyrian merchants had made full use of the Anti-Taurus passes, and the early Hittite monarch Hattusilis I (c. 1650) seems to have controlled both these routes and the Cilician Gates. But by the time of Telepinus (c. 1500) Cilicia had become the independent land of Adaniya, centred presumably on modern Adana, while the more northerly routes were included in the land of Kizzuwadna, a kingdom whose capital Kummani probably lay somewhere in the neighbourhood of modern Şar. An alliance with Kizzuwadna enabled Telepinus to make use of these routes, but shortly afterwards the rising power of Mitanni wooed Kizzuwadna from her allegiance to the Hittites. After that, control of the Anti-Taurus area frequently changed hands as the rival powers strove to assert their authority, and it seems that during this confused period Kizzuwadna managed to absorb Adaniya, thus giving her control of the Cilician Gates and the Karaman-Silifke road as well as the more northerly routes. Eventually Suppiluliumas was able to conclude a firm treaty with Kizzuwadna by which that country was left in control of the southerly routes while the Anti-Taurus area was fully incorporated into the land of Hatti. Under Mursilis Cilicia too was absorbed, with the result that when Muwatallis had to face the challenge of Egypt he could move his capital to Tarhuntassa, a town somewhere in the region of the   22 Karaman-Silifke route, in part at least because it was down that route that his contingents from western Anatolia would pass to Cilicia and so to northern Syria.

With the absorption of Kizzuwadna the boundaries of the Hittites were extended beyond their mountain homeland into the area between the Mediterranean and the Euphrates. Here the principal power had long been Aleppo, the old enemy of Hattusilis I and Mursilis I, and after his Syrian victories Suppiluliumas was quick to place his son on the throne of that town. But at the same time he had another son crowned as king of Aleppo's great rival Carchemish, and from then on it was Hittite policy to encourage the leadership of Carchemish at the expense of Aleppo. Around this bastion on the Euphrates were arranged several vassal-kingdoms, including a reorganized Mitanni to face Assyria, Ugarit and Alalah on the Mediterranean coast, and Kinza (Qadesh) and Amurru to the south to block the routes by which Egypt might seek to assert her power. This was an arrangement which held good until the final years of the Hittite Empire.

South-west, west and north-west

A good deal has been said in an earlier chapter about Hittite policy in dealing with the south-west and west. Here the natural boundary was the western edge of the Konya Plain (the Hittite 'Lower Land'), and beyond this line lay the Arzawa Lands. Here, as on the Gasgan frontier, a strong fortress-line was necessary, for despite several conquests of Arzawa and the creation of buffer-kingdoms in Hapalla (around Lakes Beyşehir and Eğridir) and Mira (the Afyon-Kütahya area) there was no permanent consolidation of Hittite power in the west. Further north lay the second great Hittite life-line, the route to the Sea of Marmara and the Troad. Along this route a policy of diplomatic tact was usually followed, for on the whole states like Ahhiyawa (the Troad?) and Wilusa (the plain of Eskişehir?) realized that a continuous flow of trade was to their advantage. What was necessary was the protection of the route from attack by the Arzawa Lands, and it was for this purpose that the Seha River Land (around Balıkesir?) was maintained and given special privileges as a buffer-state against aggression from the south.

To the north of the route lay the lands of the River Hulana (around Beypazarı), Kassiya (the valley of the Devrez Çay), and Pala and Tummana (around Kastamonu). It was the policy of Hittite monarchs to maintain these centres as a defence against the peoples further north towards the Black Sea coast. Here the country was really a continuation

of the Gasga Lands, and no permanent conquest was ever effected.
22, 2 The kingdoms of Masa (around Bolu) and Arawanna (perhaps
Safranbolu) were a constant danger to the more westerly areas, while
Tummana and Pala, situated just west of the lower Halys, were an open
target for Gasgan attack. As on the rest of the Gasga frontier, the only
possible policy was one of constant vigilance and counter-attack.

Foreign policy

On a frontier as long and diverse as the one just described no single
policy was likely to be applicable to all problems. In an ideal world
where resources are plentiful and trade flows freely both producers and
consumers realize their mutual dependence, firm agreements are
reached, and frontiers virtually cease to exist. But the Anatolian world
was far from ideal. All round the Hittite homeland were other powers
competing for the same resources, and it was the defence of these
resources, or of the routes leading to them, that may be seen to have
dictated Hittite policy. Alliances between the great powers were
possible only when two of them were faced by a threat from a third (as
when Hatti and Egypt united against Assyria). Apart from this,
international diplomacy was unlikely to have much success.

In this competitive world the Hittites had the great advantage of
being an inland 'continental' power. Although they had enemies on all
sides, it was unlikely that these enemies would ever act in unison, and in
their central position the Hittites could quickly move their armies from
one frontier to another as dangerous situations developed. Sometimes
attempts were made to solve frontier-problems by conquest (the
invasion of Mitanni by Suppiluliumas, and of the Arzawa Lands by
Mursilis are cases in point), but on the whole, Hittite kings realized that
control of what they had was enough to ensure their superiority. The
maintenance of this control depended, as we have seen, on two main
policies, diplomatic arrangements with minor buffer-states, and the use
of military force.

The army

Hittite diplomacy will be dealt with in another chapter. Here our
concern must be with the army which played such a large part in Hittite
history. This army, which on occasions numbered up to 30,000 men,
consisted of two main arms, infantry and chariots. The infantry had a
small core of permanent troops who acted as the king's personal
bodyguard and were responsible for frontier-patrols and the crushing
of rebellions. Nothing is known of their recruitment, but they were at
times supplemented by foreign mercenary troops. During the
campaigning-seasons a larger infantry-force was raised from the local
population and if necessary it was further enlarged by contingents from
vassal-kingdoms. There were also pioneers for siege-work and
messengers who may in some cases have been mounted. Apart from
29, 30 this, the horse was used only to draw the chariot – the principal
offensive weapon of the Hittites, as of all other contemporary Near
Eastern powers.

The supreme commander was the king himself, and it is clear that Hittite kings took a prominent personal part in any fighting in which their armies were involved. On occasion command could be delegated, if for instance the king were ill, or engaged in a campaign elsewhere, or if his presence were needed for cult-duties at home. In such cases the delegated commander would normally be a member of the royal family, and would bear some high-sounding court-title such as Chief Shepherd or Master of the Wine. In some areas (for instance the northern frontier and the Euphrates-line at Carchemish) special attention was necessary at all times. In such a case a royal prince could be given the title of 'king' of the area and granted a more-or-less independent command.

The system of ranks in the Hittite army is difficult to reconstruct, but it seems that minor commands were held by the lesser nobility, and that units were built up as a decimal system with officers in charge of ten, one hundred and one thousand men in a rising hierarchy of command.

Equally little is known about the payment of troops. In many cases military service was a feudal obligation and thus part of a wider system of which more will be said in another chapter. In addition, the Hittites believed in payment by results, and victory in the field was regularly followed by the distribution of booty. The dangers of this system can be seen at the Battle of Qadesh, where an easy Hittite victory was almost turned to defeat by the anxiety of the chariot-troops to plunder the enemy camp before ensuring that the field was fully theirs.

Troops in enemy territory doubtless lived off the land. The garrisons of border fortresses were presumably supported by the local population, and the same may be true of the large contingents which were frequently moved from one end to the other of the Hittite realms. But Hittite armies also had large baggage-trains of donkeys and bullock-carts which must have carried supplies as well as equipment. The principal problem both in Anatolia and in northern Syria must have been that of water-supply, and in many areas the number of routes which could have been used even by small forces is closely limited by the availability of this essential commodity.

Military equipment

In considering the equipment of Hittite armies we may well start from a recent definition of the art of warfare as an attempt 'to achieve supremacy over the enemy in three fields: mobility, fire-power, security'.[49] In the first field the principal weapon of the Hittites, as of the other powers of the time, was the light horse-drawn chariot. This vehicle was developed, probably in a Hurrian milieu, in the first half of the second millennium, and its use rapidly spread through the Middle East. A fragment of an Old Hittite relief-vessel from Boğazköy, to be dated to the seventeenth or sixteenth century, shows that by that time it had already reached central Anatolia. The perfected chariot was a remarkable skilful piece of work, light in weight and extremely manoeuvrable at speed. The body consisted of a wooden frame covered with leather. This was mounted on a wide axle on which ran spoked

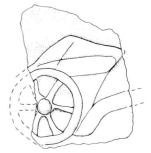

29 Hittite relief sherd showing part of a chariot. Old Hittite; from Boğazköy.

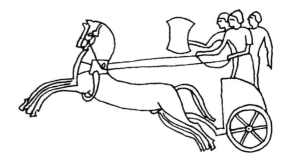

30 Hittite chariot in action. From an Egyptian relief in the Ramesseum, Thebes (after Yadin).

wooden wheels. A pole ran forward from the underside of the body, on either side of which a horse was yoked. The superiority of the Hittites in chariot-warfare lay not in their possession of this weapon (all their enemies had it too) but in their variation of the basic pattern to suit their own purposes. The ultimate problem in chariot-design is to reconcile speed and manoeuvrability with fire-power and security. For the former the designer must concentrate on lightness and such problems as the length and position of the axle; for the latter he must make his vehicle sufficiently steady for weapons to be used from it, and either give it a body which will afford some kind of protection or evolve some other means by which the warrior can protect himself. In other words, he must recognize that a charioteer has a triple function; he has simultaneously to control his chariot, fight an offensive battle, and defend himself. One answer to all this is the method adopted by Egyptian pharaohs. Rameses II at Qadesh, for instance, can be seen clad in a coat of mail for protection, and he has the reins tied round his waist to leave both hands free to operate his bow. A javelin-case is attached to the side of his chariot which, like all Egyptian chariots of the period, has its axle at the rear of the body, a position making for maximum manoeuvrability at speed. Lesser Egyptians did not share the pharaoh's all-round skill, and the normal Egyptian battle-chariot had a crew of two, a driver and a warrior armed with a bow and javelins. Clearly the Egyptians regarded chariots as highly mobile firing-platforms from which long- and medium-range missiles could be dispatched in a manner which would cause the maximum of confusion in the enemy ranks. The Hittite conception of chariot-warfare was different from this. To them a chariot formation was a heavy-weight assault force which could sweep through and demolish infantry-lines in an organized charge. So we find that in Hittite chariots the principal weapon employed was the stabbing-spear for action at close range, and that the axle was attached to the middle of the body rather than the rear. This meant that their vehicles were more liable to overturn at speed, but the sacrifice in manoeuvrability was more than counterbalanced by the increase in fire-power which resulted from it. For, because of the forward mounting of the wheels, the Hittite chariot could carry a crew of three – a driver, a warrior and a soldier who during the charge held a shield to protect the other two. Thus extra weight was given to the charge and extra man-power was available in the hand-to-hand fighting which followed it.

25

31
30

Other Anatolian powers, such as Arzawa, Ahhiyawa and even the Gasga-lands, had their chariot-forces too, but apart from references to them in Hittite texts nothing is known of their composition or armament. Indeed, much of Anatolia is such difficult country that chariots cannot have been of much assistance in battle, and they may have been used mainly for the rapid transport of kings and high-ranking officials – and for their rapid escape after a defeat, if we may judge by the number of Hittite enemies who 'fled alone', leaving their troops, and even their wives and children, to the tender mercies of the Great King.

Much less is known about the infantry divisions of the Hittite army. At the Battle of Qadesh they played a very minor part, being used mainly to protect the baggage and equipment against sudden enemy attack. But in the Anatolian hills the infantryman came into his own, and in this type of fighting too, if we can judge from the admittedly biased royal records, the Hittite army had the advantage of its opponents. This advantage seems to have been gained not so much by superior firepower as by better training and discipline, which enabled Hittite generals to move their troops over large distances making full use of the cover of natural features or of darkness, and so to achieve the element of surprise which could be so important in a successful attack. When the attack came, the marching column could quickly be turned into a battle-line which could sweep through an enemy army before it had time to organize itself. Some of the effect of the rapidly advancing Hittite line may be seen in the controlled and sinister movement of the warrior-gods in the sculpture-gallery at Yazılıkaya.   121

The principal offensive weapon of the Hittite infantryman seems to have varied according to the nature of the terrain. In northern Syria, where set battles in open country were a possibility, he was armed with a long spear, the favourite weapon of the phalanx-formation in many periods and areas. In the earlier part of the second millennium the spearhead had been attached to the shaft by a combination of a bent tang (sometimes with a 'button' at the end) bound into the shaft, and   31 slots in the blade through which the end of the shaft could be further lashed to the face of the blade. Similar tangs were used in attaching a metal spike to the other end of the spear. The primary function of this was to balance the weapon, but it could also be used in action to pierce an enemy, or it could be stuck into the ground during rest-periods while on the march. Later in the millennium the more efficient form of socketed spearhead was introduced. This was much less likely to come away from the shaft in action.

In the Anatolian hills the Hittite soldier carried the slashing-sword, a vicious-looking weapon shaped like a sickle but with the cutting-edge on the outside of the curved blade. It was not until almost the end of the second millennium that metallurgical techniques proved good enough to provide a long cutting-weapon with a straight blade. This development may have taken place in western Anatolia, if we accept that area as the original homeland of many of the 'Peoples of the Sea' who are illustrated with long-swords on Egyptian monuments. Hittite warriors also carried a short stabbing-sword or dagger which can often be seen on the sculptures. This had a hilt which was frequently

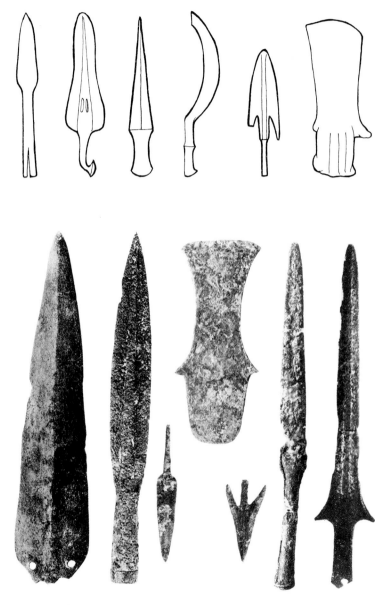

31 Weapons. *Top*: socketed spearhead from Beycesultan; tang-and-button spearhead (Middle Bronze Age) of unknown provenance; straight sword from an Egyptian relief at Medinet Habu; sickle-sword from a relief at Yazılıkaya; arrowhead from Boğazköy; shaft-hole axe from Boğazköy. *Above*: dagger from Tarsus; socketed spearhead from Tarsus; arrowhead from Mersin; flat axe from Alaca; arrowhead from Thermi; knife from Alaca; sword from Thermi. Not to scale.

crescent-shaped or (perhaps only for ceremonial use) elaborately decorated with animal heads. Often this weapon too seems to have been slightly curved, as can be seen both on sculptural reliefs and in actual examples from Boğazköy and Troy. Straight blades with a wide central flange, a strengthening device much favoured by Anatolian metalsmiths, are also to be found. In the early part of the second millennium the handle was attached to the blade by means of rivets, but later a more advanced form became popular in which the blade and hilt were cast as one piece and an inlay of wood or bone was held in position on either side of the hilt by rivets and flanged edges. In western

32

Anatolia there are naturally signs of Aegean and European influences, for instance in a dagger from Thermi with a leaf-shaped blade and a 'horned' hand-guard. The wide central flange of this weapon, however, suggests that it is locally made rather than an import. The eastward spread of similar influences can be seen in the shapes of swords on reliefs at Karabel, east of Izmir, Gavurkalesi near Ankara, and Yazılıkaya, and by the early part of the first millennium they had penetrated as far south-east as Sinjerli. Many swords and daggers had pommels of stone, bone or metal, and often these have survived when the weapons themselves have disappeared.

14, 15
121

Another weapon carried by the Hittite soldier was the axe. This took two main forms, one with a hole into which the shaft was fixed and the other a flat blade which was inserted into a split shaft and bound in position. The earliest shaft-hole axes in Anatolia are clearly linked to similar weapons in stone, but characteristically metal shapes were soon evolved. Signs of influence from widely separated areas in Anatolian examples serve to emphasize the highly international nature of metal-working in the second millennium, with smiths operating along trade-routes which were little affected by national frontiers. Axes found at Kültepe and dated to the earlier part of the millennium show a characteristically Assyrian raising of the blade above the level of the socket, and may well be linked to the presence of Assyrian trading-colonies at that site, but ribbing round the shaft-hole is a feature not only in eastern Anatolia but also in Syria, Iran and the northern Caucasus area, and cannot be directly linked with any particular element in the population. Perhaps the most famous Anatolian shaft-axe is that carried by the figure on the King's Gate at Boğazköy. In this sculpture the spikes at the rear of the shaft are really a development of the ribbing mentioned above, as can be seen in a Palestinian example of the fourteenth century from Beth-shan. The blade, however, is of a type which can be paralleled only in the Caucasus region. A curved wooden shaft and a tassel complete a weapon of which no archaeological example has yet been found.

32

The subject of flat axes without a socket is complicated by the fact that many examples may have been wood- or metalworking tools rather than weapons. However, it is clear that some at least were axes rather than broad chisels or adzes, and no doubt many were used in both peace and war. Such axes normally had projections or lugs on either side of the blade where it was fitted into the shaft, and were widely used in many parts of Anatolia. Towards the end of the Imperial period axes made of iron were beginning to come into use.

The bow was also used by Anatolian armies. Sometimes it was carried on the Egyptian pattern by chariot-troops, and it was probably the weapon of the Hittite light infantry, as well as that of the Gasga and other powers. The bow itself was of the composite type, constructed of a combination of wood and horn glued and bound to form an integrated body of great strength and power. This weapon may have been introduced to Anatolia from Mesopotamia in the Akkadian period, and it can be recognized in sculptures by its characteristic shape, which shows either ends that curve outwards or a triangular form with the bow-string forming its base. Arrowheads were of bronze, attached by a

15

32 The figure from the left-hand inner side of the King's Gate, Boğazköy. H. of complete figure 1.98 m.

tang to a body made of wood or reed, and in a great many cases with barbs at the rear corners. The quiver was of leather or bark, and probably held twenty to thirty arrows.

For personal defence Hittite soldiers wore helmets, and some at least carried shields. The best representation of a helmet is that worn by the figure on the King's Gate. It has a pointed top, flaps to cover the cheeks and neck, and a long plume which hangs down the warrior's back.

Another representation of a helmeted warrior has been found incised into the inside surface of a bowl excavated at Boğazköy and dated to c. 1400. In this case the helmet has, like that of the King's Gate figure, cheek- and neck-flaps, but in other ways it is unique in the Hittite area. The horn, crest and flowing ribbons are all to some extent reminiscent of Aegean representations,[50] and it may be that we have here a Hittite picture (the bowl is certainly of local manufacture) of an Aegean or west Anatolian warrior. Perhaps his opponent, whose picture has not been recovered, conformed more to the conventional Hittite type.

In other respects too the picture provides details which cannot at the moment be paralleled. Body-protection is provided by what looks like a sleeveless jacket, perhaps of leather, decorated with patterns of concentric circles and worn over what may be a shirt of scale-armour, with arms finished in a fringe just below the elbow. Examples of bronze armour-scales have recently been excavated at Boğazköy, and at Korucutepe two small pieces of iron may also be the remains of armour-scales. The King's Gate figure appears to have a bare chest, although the markings assumed by most people to represent the hair on his chest have also been taken by some as being intended to convey the idea of a mail shirt. The figure also wears a short kilt-like garment, which, if it corresponds to any real battle-equipment, cannot have

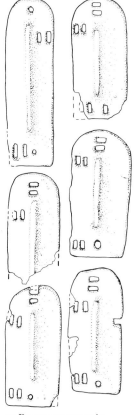

33 Bronze armour-scales from Boğazköy (after Neve). Av. H. c. 6 cm.

34 Fragments of clay vessel with incised picture of a warrior. Early Imperial period; from Boğazköy.

25 offered much protection to the wearer. Hittite infantry-troops who are represented in Egyptian pictures of the Battle of Qadesh wear an ankle-length garment which may be 'tropical kit' issued for use in the warm south-east, or a sort of 'great-coat' to be left with the baggage-train when swift action was intended. But in view of the lack of shields among the infantry it may be that in this case too the garment was in fact a long coat of mail. Hittite shields can be seen in the Egyptian pictures being carried by chariot-troops. They are of figure-of-eight shape, probably made of leather on a wooden frame, and presumably designed (despite their small size on the Egyptian reliefs) for whole-body protection. Towards the end of the millennium round shields
28 were introduced by the Sea Peoples, and they became part of the normal equipment of Neo-Hittite military units.

Fortifications

The art of fortification is an ancient one in Anatolia. The Neolithic settlement of Çatal Hüyük was defended about 6000 BC by the simple expedient (perhaps originally an architectural necessity or a defence against flood-water rather than human enemies) of building the houses without spaces between them and making all entries through the roofs. Thus any attacker was met by a solid blank wall, which was presumably high and strong enough to make his weapons ineffective. As time passed and weapons improved something stronger became necessary.
4 The settlement of Hacılar II (c. 5400) has an independent wall of mud brick between 1.5 and 3 m thick and provided with small towers which enabled the defenders to fire along the face of the wall. The slightly later (c. 5250) wall of Hacılar I is even more massive, and is built in a series of 'steps' to give a clear field for covering-fire in front of it. By
5 about 4000 BC the fortress at Mersin (Level XVI), set on a hill-top, had developed further defensive refinements. Here the mud-brick wall stood on a high terraced foundation of stone (only the towers at Hacılar had stone foundations) and the sloping face of the mound below the foundations was protected by stone slabs which made access to the wall extremely difficult. The wall itself was built in a succession of straight sections with shallow offsets where it changed direction and periodic towers for lateral fire-power. Third-millennium defences show further improvements of the same basic techniques. In the north-west especially the development of architecture in stone led to a high
6 standard of wall-construction, and the defences of Troy and Poliochni provide fine examples of sloping rubble walls crowned by a mud-brick superstructure and protected by towers and solid bastions.

If we turn now to the defensive walls of the second millennium we can see that Anatolian architects of this period had to a great extent mastered the problems of this type of construction. It is important to remember that the purpose of a defensive structure is not merely the negative one of stopping the enemy. As well as giving security it has to restore to the defenders their superiority in mobility and fire-power. This is done by placing the defenders not merely beyond the reach of the enemy but also above them and to their sides. A wall must not merely keep the enemy out, for this would lead to a siege in which the

HATTUSHA
(HATTUSAS)

0   500
          m

PROCESSIONAL WAY
TO YAZILIKAYA

CREMATIONS

BOĞAZKALE
(BOĞAZKÖY)

GATE?

GATE?

GATE

GATE

GATE?

BUYUKKAYA

BRIDGE

TEMPLE I

LOWER
CITY

GATE

GATE   KIZLARKAYA

BÜYÜK-
KALE

UPPER CITY

SOUTH CITADEL

SARIKALE   NIŞANTAŞ

TEMPLE VII

LION GATE   YENICEKALE

TEMPLE VI

TEMPLE V   KINGS
GATE

TEMPLE IV

TEMPLE II

TEMPLE III

SPHINX GATE

35 Plan of Boğazköy (after
Bittel and Neve).

defenders were inevitably at a disadvantage, but should be designed in
such a way as to provide the defenders with an answer to whatever the
enemy may try to do. Thus, although the impression one gains from the
remains of defensive walls is one of enormous thickness, the principal
requirement was height, setting the defenders above and out of reach of
the attackers. The thickness of the wall gave height with stability and
enabled the defenders to protect the weak points of the wall, the top, the
bottom, the corners and the entrances. The top of the wall had to allow
the defenders to move freely and to shoot without hindrance. Hence the
need for battlements and for a wide roadway along the wall behind
them. The bottom had to be protected from battering-rams and the
area in front of it kept clear of attackers with scaling-ladders. Hence the
development of the sloping lower face or glacis, which had the
additional advantage of causing stones dropped from above to bounce
off at unexpected angles, thus creating the maximum of havoc and
confusion in the enemy ranks. The corners of the wall were in special

36 Fragment of a Hittite vessel with modelled tower and battlements. Note the imitation wooden beams.

danger of being undermined, and Anatolian builders often approached the ideal of having no corners at all. Certainly their fortifications tended to be circular rather than rectangular, and those angles which did exist were normally covered by protective towers. The same was true of gateways, the weakest point of any fortifications. An alternative design of gateway provided for one or more right-angled bends to restrict and confuse the enemy and increase the number of directions from which defensive fire could be directed.

The most important sites that serve to illustrate these principles are Boğazköy and Troy, but additional information from sites like Alaca, Alışar, Eskiyapar, Beycesultan, Kusura, Porsuk, Meydancık, Mersin, Norşuntepe and Korucutepe, as well as Anatolian-influenced towns such as Alalah and Ugarit in north Syria, enables us to build up a clear picture of second-millennium defensive architecture in Anatolia. The walls of Boğazköy in the late Imperial period form a vast circuit over three miles long. They enclose an area which rises up from the older city in the north to a high rocky crest in the south, and just before the fall of the empire were even extended to include the steep hill known as Büyükkaya by twice bridging the deep gorge to the north of the citadel. The rough ground on which the wall was built was first raised to a constant level by heaping up a rampart of earth, sometimes 70 m wide at its foot and narrowing as it rose to provide a sloping glacis which was in places faced with dressed stone. On this rampart stood the main city-wall, a 'double-casemate' construction consisting of outer and inner skins of irregular but carefully jointed masonry connected by cross-walls and having the spaces between filled with rubble. On top of this structure, some 10 m above the earth rampart, was a further wall of mud-brick, presumably crowned by battlements such as can be seen on 36 a fragment of an ornamental vase found in the city. Rectangular towers projected from the wall at intervals of c. 30.5 m, and in some places there was an additional apron-wall built c. 7.5 m in front of the main wall and strengthened by bastions situated midway between its towers. The main gateways were flanked by large towers to which were joined the ends of both the main wall and the apron-wall. Between these

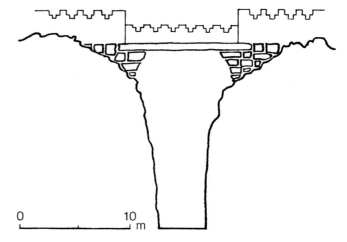

37 Wall carried on bridge across gorge at Boğazköy (after Bittel).

0   10
└────────────┘ m

towers the bronze-covered gates were set back some distance from the front faces of the towers, and secondary gates were fitted flush with their inner faces. The gates were reached by means of steep ramps parallel to the city-wall, which would force attackers to turn their flank to the defending forces. In one case at least a wall and subsidiary tower on the outer side of the ramp provided additional protection.

At the southernmost point of the city was a small gate (the 'Sphinx Gate') for pedestrian use. Here the rampart was *c.* 10.5 m high, and access to the gate from outside was by means of two staircases, one on either side of it, which were built into the paved slope of the rampart. Beneath the gate, and constructed before the rampart was built, was a corbelled postern-tunnel almost 83 m long leading to the interior of the city. A recess just inside the lower entrance was presumably a sentry-box or porter's lodge. This tunnel was certainly intended to be more than a short-cut for lazy citizens. It was, in fact, a regular feature of Hittite defensive architecture, for there are further examples in what had been the south wall of the older city, as well as at Alaca, Alışar and as far afield as Ugarit. Such tunnels may well have been used for counter-attacks, either to take the enemy by surprise or to engage him when he was on the point of collapse, but the positioning of all the Boğazköy examples beneath the southern wall,

129–30

39 Section of wall and postern-tunnel, Boğazköy (after Akurgal).

added soil

natural ground level

feet 0 50 100 150

40 Paved street running along the inner face of the city wall at the Sphinx Gate, Boğazköy.

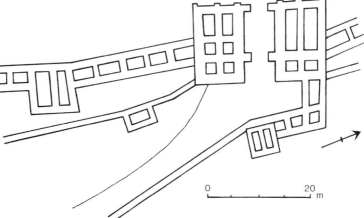

41 Plan of the King's Gate, Boğazköy (after Bittel).

on the side furthest from the constant menace of Gasgan attack, suggests that their ultimate purpose was to facilitate escape to the more friendly south when the city was on the point of being captured.

Recent excavations around the Sphinx Gate have shown that it was constructed in two main phases. In the first phase there was no apron-wall, and so when that was added alterations had to be made to the staircases and to the paved glacis on the slope of the rampart. At the same time two towers were removed from the main wall. Alterations at the King's Gate and elsewhere probably took place at the same time in a co-ordinated programme of improvement which, to judge by the unfinished state of the workings round the Sphinx Gate, had not been fully completed at the time of the final destruction of the city. Effective restoration work at the southern end of the city now gives a powerful impression of the final phase of the defensive system there. 40 41

The outer ring-wall of Boğazköy was not its sole means of defence. Inside, the city was divided into areas which could be separately defended if any section of the main wall fell to the enemy. The strongest of these areas was undoubtedly the citadel, the site of the royal palace and archives, set high above the oldest part of the town. The natural security of this site was supplemented by walls of the same type as the main city-wall. Other walls divided the rest of the city into smaller units, some of which contained fortified buildings or secondary citadels. It is easy to see how difficult it must have been to gain complete control of the city. 35

Other Anatolian sites share many of the features of the defensive architecture of Boğazköy. A wall at Korucutepe dating from the late Colony or early Old Kingdom period has an embankment topped by double stone walls supporting a mud-brick superstructure, with projecting towers at approximately 15 m intervals. In this case there are no cross-walls or casemates, and the impression one gains is that this is an earlier and simpler version of the 'Hittite' defensive wall. But the Old Hittite wall at Norşuntepe was built with interior cross-walls, and at Alışar and Karahüyük near Konya walls dating from the Colony period and built on the casemate principle show that this building method was by no means a Late Bronze Age invention. The town-wall of Alışar has no defensive towers; instead it is built in a series of 'steps' rather like the much earlier Hacılar fortress. Alaca too has a ring-wall (with towers) and a typical Hittite gateway, and although it lies south of the main Gasga border-line it may be taken as typical of a fortified border-town. A large building inside the town is usually identified as a palace and will be described in that context, but it could conceivably be a barracks for the local garrison. 73

The spread of Hittite influence to Cilicia at the time of the Old Kingdom can be seen at Mersin where a similar method of wall-construction was employed, with projecting towers to strengthen points where the wall changed direction. As at Alışar a street running along the inside of the wall aided rapid movement of troops in emergencies.

In western Anatolia the main features of defensive architecture are to be seen in the walls of Troy VI. These have been described at length in another volume of this series, and a few details must suffice here. Built 44

in several sections, the wall consisted of a mud-brick superstructure built on a high stone rampart of well-worked masonry with a pronounced batter on its outer face. Changes of direction were marked by shallow offsets or steps a few centimetres deep. These were quite independent of the jointing of the masonry, and while this technique may have been evolved to counteract the difficulty of building sloping walls along irregular ground, it results in a complete absence of corners where the masonry is weak and undermining can be usefully attempted. Towers were thus not needed to protect the angles, and their main use was for the guarding of gates, of which the principal one (the South Gate) was a passage *c.* 3.5 m wide with a tower on one side only. The other gates were constructed to a different plan which can be best illustrated by the East Gate. Here two sections of wall overlapped to leave a passage *c.* 2 m wide and 5 m long. At the inner end was a sharp bend where a door was situated. Projecting from the wall face some 27 m south of the passage was a strong rectangular tower. Thus enemy troops seeking entrance would be overlooked from both sides of the narrow passage, their movement would be impeded by the bend, and no force of any size could be gathered outside without exposing its rear to fire from the tower.

42

44

43

No system of fortifications, however well contrived, can be successful unless its defenders can maintain themselves for long periods without contact with the outside world. This means that there must be an ample supply of food and water inside the fortifications. Storage of food is relatively easy. Perhaps the best-known example is that of Troy VIIa with its large number of storage-jars sunk into the floor of almost every house. But a supply of water is a very different matter. Natural sources have to be protected, and if they do not exist, storage-tanks have to be provided. The principal source of water for Troy VI, for instance, was a well or cistern situated at the north-eastern corner of the citadel, formed by driving a shaft 4 m square and 9 m deep into the natural rock. For protection this vital source was enclosed in

45

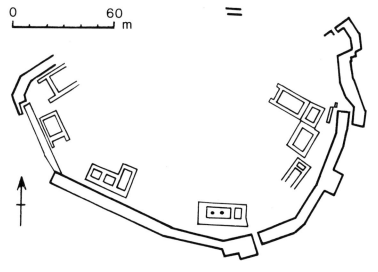

42 A section of the city wall of Troy VI, showing the characteristic vertical 'offsets', about 9 m apart, each marking a slight change in the direction of the wall.

43 The East Gate, Troy VI, showing the narrow passage formed by two overlapping sections of the wall.

44 Plan of Troy VI (after Blegen).

an enormous tower built of squared limestone blocks which rose to a height of *c.* 9 m and supported a high superstructure of mud-brick. From this tower a stone stairway led up to the interior of the citadel to provide the inhabitants with easy access to the water. Another flight of steps led to a short passage with a pivoted door on the outside of the fortress wall. This passage was narrow and easily defensible, and was presumably used as a short cut in time of peace by those who needed water for their fields and herds.

With so handy a source, and two other wells close by, the comparatively small citadel of Troy was amply provided with water. But a city the size of Boğazköy presented a much greater problem. An area such as this, with its lower end at least heavily inhabited, must have been able to draw on a large number of springs, streams or wells, a good many of which have been identified. On the citadel, and in the area known as Sarıkale, cisterns *c.* 2 m across and 2.7 m deep have been found cut into the rock. These doubtless served to hold water in times of emergency, but they were scarcely adequate for a long siege. A much later ('Late Phrygian') well has been excavated just outside the citadel. It is reached by a winding staircase of 36 steps enclosed between ashlar walls *c.* 2 m high and protected by sentry-posts at the top and a tower at the foot. It cannot, however, have been in use in the Hittite period, for it was dug exactly where a Hittite gate had stood. The problem of water-supply in the Hittite citadel has yet to be fully solved.

Finally, it should be pointed out that in seeking to defend themselves the inhabitants of second-millennium Anatolia did not put their trust

45 House in Troy VIIa, with storage vessels sunk into the floor. It is often held that the number of such vessels in the houses of Troy VIIa shows that the settlement was in a stage of siege, and that the attackers were the Greeks of the Homeric poems.

46 The pillars set up outside the South Gate, Troy VI. Probably originally six in number, they may well have had some sort of protective function.

solely in stone and mud-brick. No city, however strong, could stand without the protective aid of supernatural powers. At Boğazköy the King's Gate, the Lion Gate and the Sphinx Gate all have their carved portal-figures designed to keep evil influences and evil men at bay. The sphinxes on the main gate at Alaca perform the same function. At Troy the sculptural technique is poorer, but the apotropaic power is doubtless equally effective. Here outside the South Gate rectangular pillars, probably originally six in number,[51] were set up along the face of the gate-tower. These pillars have unfortunately been broken off, and so it is not clear whether their upper parts were carved or not, but their purpose seems clear. Without doubt they are to be linked with the raised altar inside the gate-tower, and with a long narrow building on the opposite side of the gate in which throughout the life of the sixth settlement burnt sacrifices were offered to the divine powers whose symbols or images stood just across the road. A similar pillar was erected outside the western gate of the citadel. But although these monoliths, aided by the stout walls, were able to deal with any human attacks, they could not cope with the superior power of the earthquake which in the view of the excavator devastated Troy VI and toppled large sections of its masonry to the ground.

47 Detail of the Lion Gate, Boğazköy (see also ills. 126–7).

73

5

Society and administration

Although our evidence for Anatolian social and political structure comes mainly from the archives of a city-dwelling upper class, it is important to remember that the basic unit of Anatolian society has long been – and to a large extent still is – the village. Hittite texts offer hundreds of place-names preceded by the determinative usually translated 'town' or 'city', but it is clear that this determinative was applied to any collection of houses, however small, and that most of the 'towns' were in fact only villages. Archaeological surveys have shown that towns of any size were comparatively few in number, and a city on the scale of Hattusas was wholly exceptional. The society in which the vast majority of the inhabitants of second-millennium Anatolia lived was not an urban one. Life was centred on the small agricultural communities in which people were born, communities which were self-contained, self-sufficient, and in their essentials unaltering from year to year and down the centuries. It is easy to see that despite the many changes of government which have taken place in the intervening period the Anatolian village today is much like its predecessor over three thousand years ago. So in many cases where information is scanty or non-existent a study of modern village life[52] can lead to a fuller understanding of the life and organization of a small Hittite community.

Village society

Every village had its own cultivable territory, separated from that of neighbouring villages by uncultivated 'no-man's-land'. On its territory each village grew its crops and fed its animals, and within that territory it was responsible for the maintenance of law and order and the protection of strangers. Much of the village land was held in common, but some at least could be leased to individual villagers ('men of the tool' in the Hittite Law Code) in return presumably for their services to the community as craftsmen. These land-holders had also to devote some time to labour on public works such as wells and irrigation channels.

The most important figures in village life were the Elders, who formed a governing body and were probably the senior heads of households in the community. These households were patrilineal in structure, and in them the father exercised a great deal of authority. He not only 'gave' his daughters to their prospective husbands but could even give a son to another household whose son he had killed. Wives, however, were not regarded as mere possessions of their husbands, but seem to have retained some vestiges of a more independent position. A woman of free birth, for instance, who married a slave, kept her status as a free woman. Wives had at least some say in the disposal of their daughters in marriage, and in certain circumstances (admittedly very obscure) they could disown their sons and even divorce their husbands. Although the normal marriage-arrangement was that a man 'took' a wife and 'made a house and children' with her (the phraseology suggests nuclear rather than extended families as social units, and this is not incompatible with the archaeological evidence) it was possible in some cases for a woman to remain in her father's house after marriage. On the other hand the custom of levirate marriage, by which a widow was married to her late husband's brother, father or other surviving male relative, can only have been acceptable in a society where male primacy was a recognized feature.

Mention has just been made of slaves, and there is no doubt that slavery did exist in Hittite society. Yet it is well-nigh impossible to say what proportion of the community consisted of slaves, or what part, if any, they played in the village economy. In the Imperial period at least slaves were the property of their masters, who had the power of life and death over them, but in the Old Kingdom, as reflected in the Law Code, slaves had legal rights and were able to own property. It seems likely that they were employed mainly as servants to the rich. Much more important in a village context were the large numbers of people deported from conquered countries and settled on land in Hittite territory. These deportees were not assigned to individual owners, but remained under the control of the state. The extra man-power they provided was increasingly needed in the Imperial period as increased productivity was demanded at the same time as Hittite citizens were more and more required for military duties.

Another way in which the state imposed its authority on village life can perhaps be seen in those sections of the Law Code in which prices are fixed for a large number of commodities and wages regulated for many services. Unfortunately we do not possess the private documents which would enable us to see what effect, if any, the edicts of the Hittite Prices and Incomes Board had on everyday life. We also lack evidence for the possible effects of inflation on a system of fixed prices. On the whole it is difficult to believe that the ordinary day-to-day transactions of village life could have been rigorously controlled by government policy, and evidence from Mesopotamia, where there is ample documentation to show that 'law-codes' represented a ruler's pious hopes rather than his firmly enforced prescriptions, serves to confirm this impression.

The Government: the Old Kingdom

What was the nature of the government which was superimposed on the village system, and was in many ways alien to it? In the period preceding the rise of Hattusas Anatolia had consisted of a large number of 'city-states', each with its own fairly limited territory and its own central palace organization, and the rise of Hattusas did not lead to any fundamental changes, but was rather an extension and elaboration of what was by then a traditional Anatolian system. All effective power was in the hands of a limited number of families or clans who formed an aristocracy. Among these the most important was the 'Great Family' which provided the king and the highest officers of state, whose main function was, if one can judge by their titles, to supervise the various departments of the royal household. The other members of the aristocracy combined their role as warriors with administrative duties in the palace departments, and were collectively known as the 'fighting men and servants of the king'. As a body they also formed the *pankus* or 'whole body of citizens'. This functioned primarily as a law-court, and members were entitled to trial by their peers. Even the king was liable to be brought before it, although there is no evidence that this ever actually happened. It was moreover summoned by Hattusilis I to hear his proclamation of his successor, if not in fact to approve or veto his choice. This has suggested to many that the *pankus* was a relic of an Indo-European institution, to be compared for instance with the Teutonic *teuta*,[53] and that the position of king was, as in other Indo-European societies, originally an elective one. But it has to be stressed that if this is so most traces of it had disappeared long before the period of our earliest evidence, for the *pankus* under Hattusilis I and Telepinus was an almost completely powerless body. There is nothing to indicate that Hattusilis required its approval for his choice of successor, and on the only occasion on which we hear of it functioning as a court its decision was arbitrarily overruled by the king.

49   Closely connected with the position of king was that of queen (*tawanannas*), and here there are many features which suggest that this lady did not hold her title merely because she was the king's consort. She retained her position after the death of her husband, and often took part in the governing of the country. This has been seen as a relic of original Anatolian matriarchy, later joined by marriage to an Indo-European system of kingship, but there is no real evidence for this.[54] More probably the queen held her position primarily because of her religious duties, and it is possible that she owed her importance originally to a system of brother-sister marriage within a closed royal family. But again if this is true it must have ceased to be the case long before the emergence of the Hittite kingdom. It has also been suggested[55] that in the Old Hittite period the *tawanannas* was not the king's wife, but on the whole the evidence does not support this.

Members of the aristocracy were bound by oaths of loyalty to the king, and in return for their services were given grants of land. Thus the elements of a 'feudal' system were present from the earliest days, although the word would be shunned by students of medieval western Europe, who can see no trace of the elaborate pyramid of obligations which is characteristic of genuine feudalism. The control of conquered territory was given at first to members of the royal family, and then with the extension of Hittite authority increasingly to governors and military commanders drawn from the other aristocratic families. These officials

48–9 Impressions of royal seals. *Far left*: seal of Tudhaliyas IV (see also ill. 120); *left*: seal of Suppululiumas and Queen Tawanannas.

were expected to work with the Elders of their districts and to supervise the administration of justice, the due performance of festivals and the general welfare of the people, but many of them were doubtless more concerned with furthering their personal interests. In the Old Kingdom period these 'barons' were a constant threat to royal authority, especially when a king died and his successor had yet to establish himself firmly on the throne, and it was only under Telepinus that their power was defined and curtailed, and a regular rule of royal succession established.

The Government: the Imperial period

The years between 1500 and 1400 saw vast changes in the organization of the state and the position of the Hittite king. By the Imperial period the monarch was a remote and absolute figure, the *pankus* had been abolished, and the 'feudal' organization had become much stronger. The reasons for these changes are still rather obscure. Some of them may be connected with the increasing importance of the light horse-drawn chariot as a weapon of war, for this was an expensive piece of equipment, the efficient operation of which required full-time training of both horse and man. In order to cope with this there was a great enlargement of the baronial class, supported by grants of state-owned land and bound by feudal ties to the king. Other changes may be due to the spread of Mesopotamian ideas of kingship into Anatolia through increasing Hurrian influence, and closer contact with Egypt may also have had its effect. But in many ways the differences were not so much foreign importations as developments of the old system made necessary by the increasing complexity of the expanding empire. Thus the system of local governors, drawn from the aristocracy and bound by personal oath to the king, was extended to include vassal-rulers of conquered states, who were obliged to pay homage to the Great King, to fight in his wars, and to pay a yearly tribute. In some cases the larger conquered states were given an appearance of independence by a diplomatic fiction which classed them as protectorates rather than vassals, but foreign policy always remained in the hands of the Hittite king.

30

Occasionally, on the Gasgan frontier for instance or in northern Syria, the oldest system of all was retained, under which royal relatives were appointed as local kings to ensure the loyalty of these vital areas.

The position of a vassal was carefully defined by an elaborate treaty, introduced by a historical preamble which detailed the graciousness of earlier Hittite kings towards the vassal's ancestors, and rounded off by a long list of the gods whose wrath would descend on anyone foolish enough to break the contract. Similarly elaborate treaties were made with the other Great Powers of the day, based on the equality and 'brotherhood' of the participants, and guaranteeing such matters as united action against common enemies and the succession, on the death of either party, of his legitimate heir. Inter-dynastic marriages were a common political device, and Hittite princesses were frequently sent off to a future of doubtful marital bliss in order to cement an alliance or ensure a vassal's loyalty. Behind all this lay an international Civil Service system by means of which the powers kept in touch with each other, and through which mutually acceptable arrangements could be made. Exchanges of gifts were common, and monarchs kept up a regular correspondence with their 'brothers', as well as with the subordinate rulers of vassal-states.

Other areas

Although what has been said in this chapter applies primarily to the Hittites and to those parts of Anatolia which were controlled by them, there is little doubt that much of it is equally true of other areas. Village life in the west, for instance, cannot have been different in essentials from that in central Anatolia, and there is nothing to suggest that Arzawa was not controlled by a ruling family and palace organization basically similar to that of Hatti. The relationship between Arzawa proper and the other Arzawa lands is not at all clear. It may have been one of vassaldom, and it can be seen that the royal families of the lesser states were closely linked to Arzawa by a series of dynastic marriages. In the international field Arzawa suffered from being rather on the periphery of the Middle Eastern world, but the king of Arzawa was eager to have himself admitted to the brotherhood of Great Kings. Unfortunately in his case his civil service was unable to cope with Akkadian, the international language of the day, and when he wrote to his 'brother' in Egypt the correspondence had to be conducted in Hittite, the lesser language of internal Anatolian diplomacy. Doubtless this defect would soon have been remedied had the king succeeded in establishing himself as an international figure.

44   Little can be said of the social and political organization of the far north-west except that the site of Troy looks very much like the residence of a feudal lord and his barons, and that therefore the basic patterns detailed above may also be applied to this area. Elsewhere, in Azzi-Hayasa for instance, what little evidence we have suggests that the situation was not greatly different, while in the more remote parts some sort of tribal organization probably prevailed throughout the second millennium.

6

Daily life in Late Bronze Age Anatolia

Streets and houses

Excavations at second-millennium sites in Anatolia have yielded a fair amount of information on the conditions in which people lived and worked. At Boğazköy, Alaca, Beycesultan, Tarsus, Maşat, Norşuntepe and Tepecik sufficiently large areas have been cleared to give a reasonable picture of the layout and domestic architecture of an Anatolian town. It can be seen at once that some attention was paid to over-all town-planning. Streets had a strong tendency to be straight if the lie of the land allowed it, and were often well finished with a surface of coarse gravel. In an area where almost every site was on sloping ground, systems of terracing were constantly necessary, and a great deal of attention had to be given to problems of drainage and water-disposal. Many streets had large drainage-channels, painstakingly built and roofed with stone slabs, running down the middle and connected to lesser channels or clay pipes which carried dirty water into them from the houses on either side. The whole system strongly suggests an organized municipal administration.

50, 51, 56

50 The 'North Street' area of Beycesultan II, facing east. The surface of the street can be clearly seen. On the left is a building of megaron type with circular hearth, approached through a room in which a paved area may have been used for ablutions. Beyond the east end of the megaron lie the grain-shop and tavern. To the right of the street lie the stables.

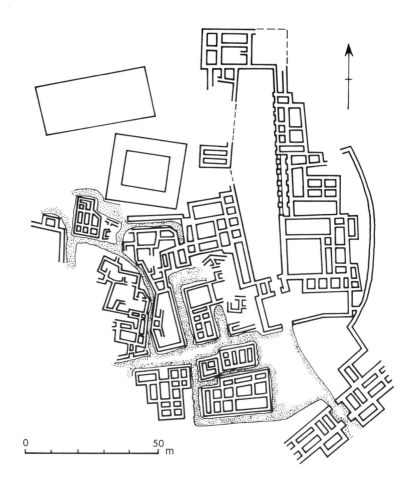

51 Plan of excavated area, Alaca II (after Koşay and Akok).

0   50

m

Within the areas bordered by the streets there is often much less evidence of planning. Houses were of very varied shapes and sizes, and the principal impression can often be one of complete irregularity. Builders in Hittite territory, although they invariably adopted a vaguely rectangular plan, seem not to have believed in accurate right angles or in a regular layout of rooms. Their simple object was to utilize all the space that was available on the site. Sometimes a standard house-pattern can be seen. At Boğazköy, for instance, just outside the temenos-wall of the main temple, there is a group of houses, each consisting of a courtyard with two rooms behind, built back-to-back and opening into parallel lanes. In other cases all that can be said is that there was a principal room or courtyard with a number of lesser rooms joined to it. It should be stressed that the courtyard, if there was one, was not normally placed centrally as a formal feature, but was much more a front yard used for domestic purposes.

In the south-west, at Beycesultan, a slightly different pattern can be seen. This consisted of a courtyard, off which lay a 'porch-room' with a wide opening supported on wooden posts. Beyond the porch-room were inner rooms whose layout differed from house to house. Other houses at the same site had the form of a megaron or hall-and-porch,

54

55

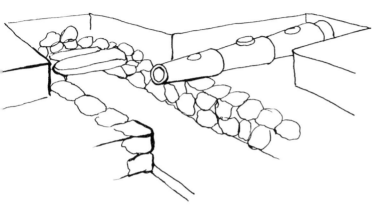

52 Part of the drainage-system at Alaca (after Koşay and Akok).

53 Drainage-channel running along the front of Temple I, Boğazköy.

56 with subsidiary rooms along one side. Houses of megaron type have also been found at Klazomenai.

The standard building-material was mud-brick on a foundation of stones, but in areas where stone was freely available it could be used for the lower parts of walls as well, or be employed as a facing on the surface of mud-brick walls, or even replace mud-brick completely. Wattle-and-daub was popular in coastal areas, and timber reinforcement, both horizontal and vertical, was, as in other periods, a characteristic feature. The value of such reinforcement as a cushion against earth-tremors was certainly recognized by Anatolian builders. Upper stories of mainly wooden construction were sometimes added to

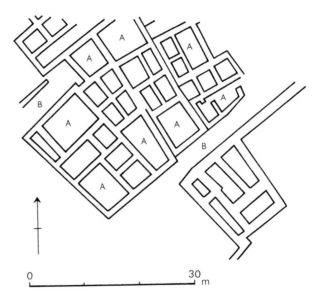

0   30
                                              m

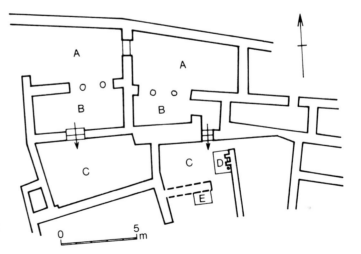

54 Plan of houses north of Temple I, Boğazköy, A, courtyard; B, lane (after Naumann).

55 Houses in Area 'A', Beycesultan Level II. A, courtyard; B, porch-room; C, inner room; D, hearth; E, sink (after Lloyd).

56 The 'Little Palace' area at Beycesultan, Level II (after Lloyd).

0   5
                  m

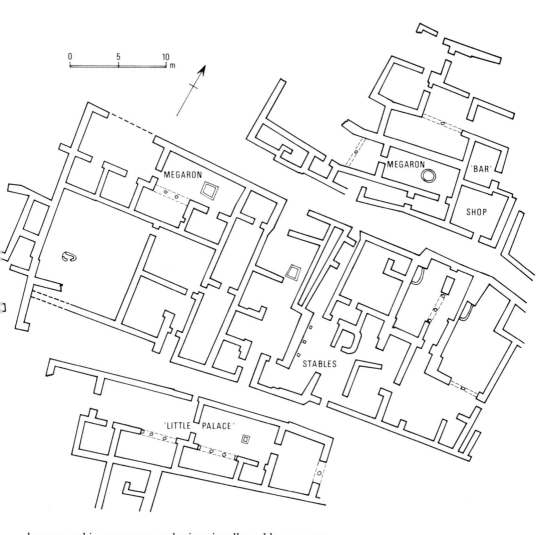

houses, and in some cases a sloping site allowed basement store-rooms to be constructed at one end of a building, with the living-quarters presumably above. Floors were either of beaten earth or finished with plaster, pebbles or flagstones. Windows, if they existed at all, were small and high up in the walls, and roofs were flat, composed of brushwood and dried mud supported on wooden beams. Interior arrangements were fairly rudimentary. Hearths and ovens were of course a necessity, and stone sinks connected to drains occur. Paved areas within some houses may have been wash-rooms or toilets, and clay baths in sizes suitable for adults and children, some with built-in seats, have been found. The more well-to-do may have had such articles as wooden beds, tables and chairs, but for the most part people worked, ate and slept at floor level. Items of simple domestic equipment, for instance brushes in the form of clay cylinders pierced lengthwise to hold wooden handles and on one side to hold bristles, are sometimes to be found.

58

67

59

The houses of lesser citizens, though normally self-contained units,
were usually built together in blocks enclosed by roads or lanes. Free-
standing houses also occurred, which must in many cases have been
occupied by people of greater wealth or higher position. A house such
as that near the Lion Gate at Boğazköy probably belonged to a fairly
well-to-do private citizen, but other buildings in the upper part of the
city were built on outcrops of natural rock and may have been 'castles'
in which members of the ruling class lived.[56] Such buildings were
adapted to the positions they occupied, and again it is difficult to see
any regular pattern. The building on Nişantepe manages to preserve a
fairly rectangular form, and with rooms opening off three sides of a
courtyard and probably a staircase to an upper storey, it offers a rather
more formal plan than the houses in the lower town. On Sarıkale there
was a building which fairly closely resembles our idea of a castle – a
tower-like 'keep' on the highest and most precipitous part of the rock
approached by a tortuous path through an outer system of multiple
defensive walls. The castle in Yenicekale is irregular in outline, and
little can be said of it except that it consisted of several rooms and was
approached through a walled courtyard built on the neck of rock which
connected the site to level ground. The reconstruction offered is of an
extremely tentative nature.

51

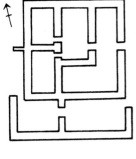

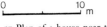

0   10 m

57 Plan of a house near the
Lion Gate, Boğazköy (after
Naumann).

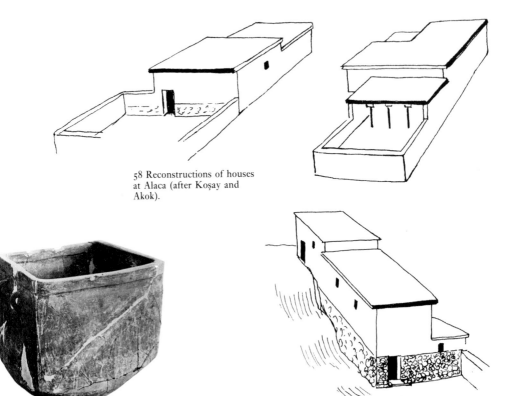

58 Reconstructions of houses
at Alaca (after Koşay and
Akok).

59 Bath-tub from Alaca.
H. 76 cm. L. 73.5 cm.

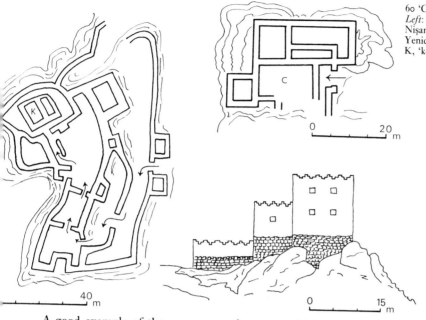

60 'Castles' at Boğazköy.
Left: Sarikale; *top right*: Nişantepe; *bottom right*: Yenicekale. C, courtyard; K, 'keep' (after Naumann).

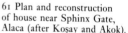

A good example of the more pretentious type of house has been excavated just inside the main gate at Alaca. The building is constructed on a stone foundation, and the floors are raised above the level of the street outside. The stones of the foundation which show above street level are alternately light and dark in colour, and provide a very rare instance of attention to external decoration in domestic architecture. (The lower part of a house-wall at Korucutepe is also faced with flat stones set on edge; but in this case there is no sign of colour-change, and the stones are for protection rather than decoration.) The plan of the Alaca building is formal, though by no means completely symmetrical, with a recessed central porch on the

61

61 Plan and reconstruction of house near Sphinx Gate, Alaca (after Koşay and Akok).

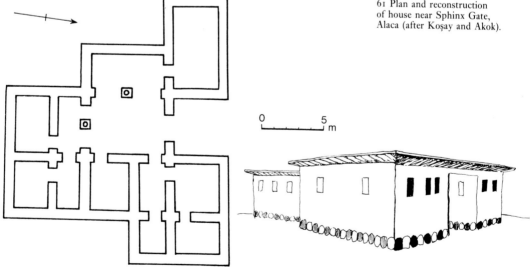

85

north side leading to a central court off which the rooms of the house open. From its size and position the house must have been occupied by an important local dignitary.

Elsewhere less can be said about larger houses. At Beycesultan the so-called 'Little Palace' consists of two local courtyard-and-porch-room units joined side by side, with the addition of a sort of ante-room at one end. At Tarsus a two-storeyed building built round three sides of a court seems to have been used as an official residence or for administrative purposes. Apart from an outer court and a large inner room there is little that can be said about its architectural details.

Accommodation inside individual houses may sometimes have been provided for animals as well as humans. At Tarsus, in a large house built on a sloping site, which has been described as a 'governor's residence' on the strength of the number of clay seal-impressions found there, a semi-basement room was provided with a large manger the dimensions of which at first suggested to the excavators that it had been

56

62

63

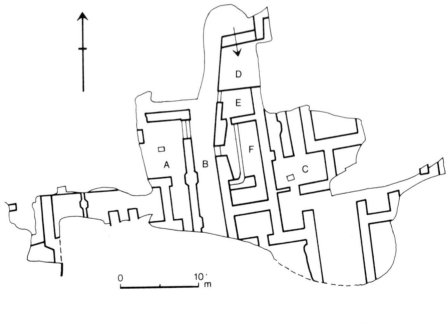

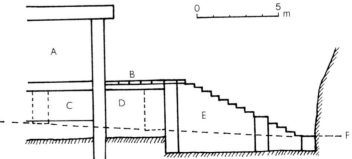

62 Plan of houses at Tarsus. A, courtyard; B, street; C, 'Governor's Residence'; D, ramp with steps; E, harness-room; F, 'manger-room' (after Goldman).

63 Section of 'manger-room' area, Tarsus. A, upper living room; B, paved terrace; C, 'manger-room'; D, harness-room; E, ramp; F, street level (after Goldman).

used by donkeys. If this is so (the excavators later opted for human occupation[57]) the animals descended by means of a step from the street and crossed a room (a harness-room?) to reach their living-quarters, and the roof of the harness-room was paved with stone to provide a terrace for the inhabitants of the house above the stable. At Beycesultan a considerable area was recognizable as stabling accommodation for horses, complete with mangers, tethering-posts, grooms' quarters and even the remains of straw on the floors.

64 Part of the stable-area of Beycesultan II. The holes seen in the foreground mark the position of posts to which horses were tethered. In other parts of the area hoof-marks were preserved in decayed straw bedding.

Shops

If we turn now to the commercial life of these settlements, one- or two-room units opening on to the streets at Alaca have been taken to be shops or workshops, while at Beycesultan there is a fine example of a grain-shop or food-store. This was a rectangular room, *c.* 5 m by 4 m, opening directly off a main street. Standing along the walls on either side of the room were large storage-jars, some almost 1.5 m in height, which were for the most part about half full of wheat, barley or lentils. In one corner of the room a small stair led up to a sort of 'cat-walk' which ran round the room and gave access to the jars from above. A grain-bin of brick and wood was built against the back wall. For some unexplained reason, a large amount of pottery, some of it nested in matching sets of six, was also found in the room. The proprietors may well have sold crockery as well as grain.

66

Immediately behind the grain-store, and approached by a side door, lay a smaller room, about 4 m by 3 m in which the area opposite the door was largely taken up by a 'bar' of mud-brick, behind which were

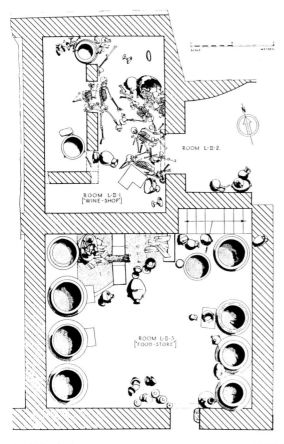

ROOM L-II-2.

ROOM L-II-1
['WINE-SHOP']

ROOM L-II-3
['FOOD-STORE']

65–6 The food-store at
Beycesultan II, and the
wine-shop behind.

67 The stone sink in the 'snack bar' of Troy VIIa. The bottom is formed of thin stone slabs and the sides of similar stone slabs standing on edge and rising about 15 cm above the level of the bottom. A rectangular hole in the wall of the building, seen at the bottom left-hand corner of the sink, allows water to drain into the street outside.

two storage-jars partly sunk in the floor, and a pile of drinking-cups in one corner. In a large earthenware basin on the customers' side of the bar was a collection of seventy-seven knuckle-bones and thirty-one crescent-shaped terracotta objects which are elsewhere very common and are usually taken to be loom-weights. In this case they had presumably been used in the same way as thrifty card-players of today use matches. Sprawled around the floor were eight human skeletons. 65 From the position of the bones it could be seen that their owners had not, like the Archpoet, simply decided *in taberna mori*, but had been clubbed to death elsewhere and afterwards hurriedly deposited in the room.

Another interesting glimpse of Late Bronze Age catering arrangements is to be seen at Troy, where a building of period VIIa, 67 immediately inside the main South Gate, shows features which suggest that it was something more than a simple dwelling-house. A wide doorway gave access from the street to a small hall-way, off which opened a large room containing a central raised hearth, and beside it a saddle-quern fixed in a tilted position on a stand of crude brick and clay so that flour ground in it would fall into a clay-lined basin in the floor. Against the street-wall was a kitchen sink of stone slabs with a well-built drain which emptied outside the building. Next to the sink were the lower parts of two fire-boxes which had probably originally supported a baking-oven. Next to this, and nearest the city-wall, were storage-bins containing remains of carbonized wheat. All this suggests that the building was used for cooking and food-preparation, and it is a happy fancy of the excavators that a counter was placed across the wide front doorway, and that the establishment was a 'snack-bar' where Trojan heroes, tired by their efforts against the Homeric Greeks, could pause in safety for a beer and a sandwich before reporting to King Priam at the central palace.[58]

Palaces

Of this palace itself no trace now remains, and we have to turn elsewhere for information on royal residences. The 'Burnt Palace' at Beycesultan dates from the Middle Bronze Age and so is too early to be included in this survey. In the Late Bronze Age the site of this palace was occupied by a walled enclosure *c.* 91 m across, but the buildings excavated within this area seem domestic in character and have already been described in that context. In the south-east, a palace area has been excavated at Tilmen Hüyük, near Islâhiye. This was certainly used in the Late Bronze Age, but its primary construction took place in the Middle Bronze Age, and once again it is too early for a description to be given here. The same is true of the palaces of central Anatolia which flourished during the Colony-period – Kültepe, Acem Hüyük and Karahuyük-Konya.

This brings us to the most important palace of all, the residence of the rulers of the Hittite Empire, set on the rocky eminence of Büyükkale at Boğazköy. The choice of this hill as a palace-site was an obvious one. It towers above the old city and is protected by sheer cliffs on the eastern and northern sides, while to the south and west it could easily be strengthened by man-made fortifications. The top of the rock forms a sloping roughly trapezoidal plateau *c.* 220 m by 150 m in extent. The earliest traces of habitation go back to the end of the third millennium, and by the Colony period it had acquired a substantial defensive wall of mud-brick on a stone foundation. A hundred years after its destruction by Anittas of Kussara it was reoccupied (*c.* 1650 BC) by Hattusilis I, the founder of the Old Kingdom. Unfortunately later building operations have destroyed most of the evidence for structures of this period, and only a few traces of relatively minor buildings have been recovered. About 1400, at the beginning of the Imperial period, there was a considerable amount of rebuilding, most of which is again very poorly preserved. Inside a new defensive wall the

68 View to the north from Büyükkale, the citadel of Hattusas (Boğazköy). The deep gorge which protects the citadel is in the centre of the picture, with the rock Büyükkaya, which in the final years of the Empire was brought within the city boundaries, on the right (see also p. 65).

68–71

lower end of the plateau was occupied by a succession of fairly small
free-standing buildings, most of which seem to have been domestic in
character. At the upper end, closest to the cliffs and farthest from the
gateway at the south-western corner, stood the palace itself. It
consisted of a central courtyard surrounded by a colonnade off which
the royal apartments opened. Other buildings were erected round the
edge of the plateau, and since the area available was too small to support
the rising aspirations of the Hittite monarchy it was extended on the
east and west sides by the addition of huge terraces of cyclopean
boulders on which the foundations of the walls and outer buildings
rested. Unfortunately most of the details have again been destroyed by
later building operations.

Just after 1300 BC Muwatallis transferred the seat of government
further south to Tarhuntassa, and Hattusas became for a short time a
mere provincial capital. To this period may be dated the modest
domestic buildings on the lower plateau known as level IVa. Later,
under Urhi-Teshub, the palace was at least partly destroyed, and his
successor Hattusilis III seized the opportunity for a large-scale
reconstruction which was not completed until the reign of Tudhaliyas
IV. This is Büyükkale III, sufficient of which has been preserved to
give a reasonably good picture of the thirteenth-century palace of the
Hittite kings.

71

During this period the palace buildings were extended to fill the
whole of the plateau. In order to make the maximum use of the space
available the rock-terraces of the previous period were reserved for
building purposes and new defensive walls were founded on extremely
difficult ground further down the steep slopes. The main public
entrance to the citadel was still at the south-west corner. It had, like the

71 (*opposite*) Plan of
Büyükkale (after Bittel).

city gates, two doorways and outside flanking towers, and was reached by means of a fairly narrow ramp suitable only for pedestrian traffic. Once inside the gate, the visitor found himself in an entrance-court of irregular shape across which a path of red marble slabs led through a portal to a larger court; long, open colonnades formed three sides of this, uniting the individual buildings round the court into a single architectural unit. On the far side was another gateway, an elaborate triple structure with guard-rooms or porters' cubicles on either side. This led to a further courtyard where again open colonnades linked the façades of imposing buildings. Beyond this lay yet another similar court round which, on the highest and most spectacular part of the site, lay the residential quarters of the royal family.

The king himself did not need to use the public entrance. He could leave the middle courtyard by a door or gate at its south-eastern corner, and proceed from there by way of a second gate in the citadel-wall provided with an outer ramp with a width and gradient suitable for chariots. For the benefit of servants and minor officials who lived in the lower town there was a third entrance, a much less grandiose structure which led via a ramp or staircase from the southern end of the western wall to the terraces behind the main palace-buildings. Finally a paved road ran along the inside of the southern wall between the two main gateways. This road could be closed at two points by doorways, and although the paving suggests something of greater importance, it must have been a mere short-cut for palace functionaries.

When we turn to the purpose for which individual buildings in the palace-complex were built our path is beset with difficulties. The sloping nature of the site, for instance, is such that buildings were entered from the courtyards at first-floor level, so that surviving walls give us only the plans of basement rooms. Worse than this, some of the most important buildings on the highest part of the rock have been so completely destroyed by later clearances that only very slight traces of them remain. Of the structures to the east of the middle courtyard, for instance, virtually nothing survives, while in the innermost court only the barest traces, such as beddings for the bases of the pillars of the colonnade, cut into the bare rock of the plateau, give an indication of what must once have stood there.

70 Büyükkale from the north. The citadel-rock is on the upper right of the picture, with Büyükkaya on the left.

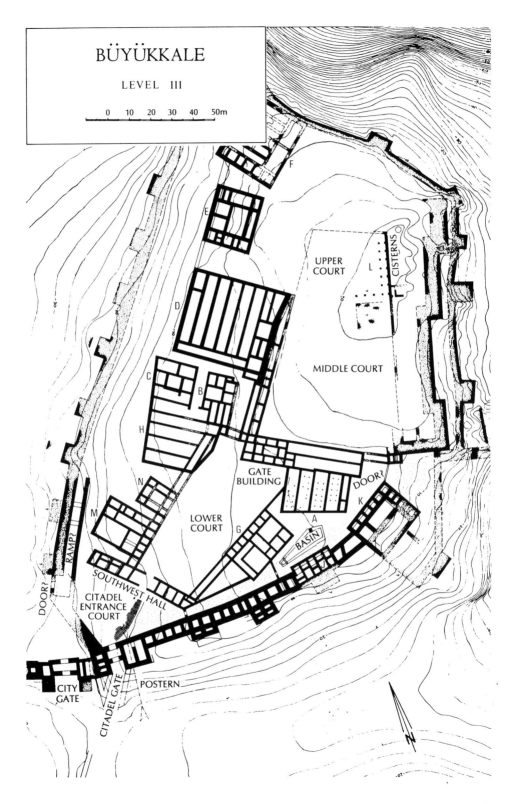

BÜYÜKKALE

LEVEL III

0   10   20   30   40   50m

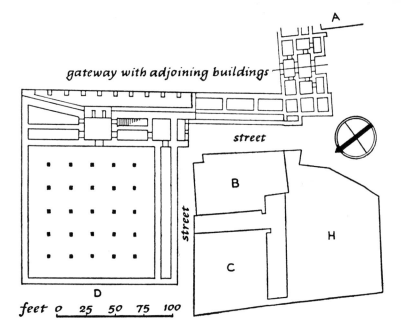

gateway with adjoining buildings

street

street

B

H

C

D

feet 0 25 50 75 100

72 Plan of Building D,
Büyükkale (after Akurgal).

Apart from these difficulties the function of even well-preserved buildings is often more or less impossible to determine. But in some instances sufficient evidence survives to permit reasonable guesses to be made. The two buildings west of the upper courtyard (Buildings E and F) are almost certainly domestic in character. The building to the south of the middle courtyard (Building A) contained large numbers of clay tablets, and presumably housed the royal archive and library. Other tablets were found in Buildings E and K, but it has been suggested that the library was temporarily split up because of the continuing process of rebuilding.[59] Building D, on the western side of the same court, has a basement level which consists almost entirely of long narrow rooms. The walls of these may well have served as supports for rows of pillars at courtyard level. These pillars in their turn would have supported an upper storey and formed the principal feature of an audience-hall over 30 m square. This hall could be entered either directly from the middle courtyard or via a narrow lane which led through a door from the north-western corner of the lower courtyard to a side entrance at basement level. From this entrance a staircase brought visitors to the vestibule of the hall, and so into the royal presence, without the need for them to enter the middle court.

Not all the buildings in the palace complex were for secular use. Building C, which lay rather off the beaten track towards the western

72

73 Reconstruction of the east side of the palace at Alaca (after Koşay and Akok).

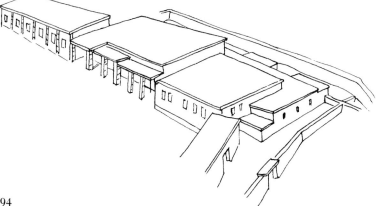

94

edge of the plateau, may well have had a ritual purpose. More will be said of this in the chapter on religion.

At Alaca, only a few miles north of Boğazköy, the largest building has several features which are sufficiently reminiscent of the structures in Büyükkale for it to be claimed as a palace. The entrance to this building faces the main city-gate across a wide open square, and leads by way of an outer court and a double gateway to a long, narrow courtyard *c*. 76 m by 15 m in extent. At the centre of the right-hand side of this court is an open colonnade, and the pattern of the pillars is picked up and emphasized by means of pilasters on at least some of the walls on either side of the court. The principal room lies just to the right of the double gateway, and is entered by way of two narrower rooms from a door at the southern end of the colonnade. Its size, *c*. 12 m square, suggests that if it was roofed (and its position next to the main court makes it unlikely that it was also a courtyard) the roof would have needed internal support, making this another 'pillar-hall' like the one in Büyükkale. Other rooms are presumably domestic or administrative in character, and one, at the north-western corner, may have been a shrine.

More recently another palatial building has been excavated at Maşat, about sixty-five miles north-east of Hattusas. The central feature of this was, as usual, a large colonnaded courtyard, *c*. 41 m by 36 m in

51, 73

74

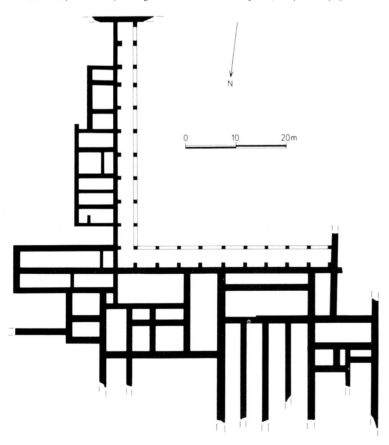

74 Plan of the Hittite palace at Maşat (after Özgüç).

95

extent. Round this were doubtless arranged the official apartments of the palace, but as at Hattusas these were entered at first floor level, and what has been preserved gives us the plan of only the basement rooms. Many of these were clearly used for storage, and in two of them clay tablets have survived, fallen from the 'official' level when the palace was destroyed by fire. Thus the palace contains the first Hittite archive known outside Hattusas itself. There was also an upper storey, constructed mainly of wood, and interior walls were finished with cream or pink plaster, or with a reddish-white wash. Some walls were decorated with thin red lines four or five feet above floor level, but there is no sign of more elaborate wall-paintings. The Maşat palace is particularly important because its destruction can be dated to about 1400. It thus gives us our earliest clear example of the use of the colonnaded courtyard, and provides us with information on Hittite palace-architecture dating from a period when the capital has little or no evidence to offer.

Agriculture

If we turn now to the everyday life of most ordinary citizens of second-millennium Anatolia, it can be seen that for most people it was concerned almost exclusively with agriculture. Although not enough work has been done on the ecology of the area, sufficient is known from textual and archaeological sources to give a fairly clear picture of the fauna and flora both wild and domesticated. The main crops were emmer-wheat and barley; but peas, beans, onions, flax, figs, olives, grapes, apples and possibly pears and pomegranates also were grown. Cattle, pigs, goats, sheep, horses, donkeys, dogs and perhaps water-buffalo were kept, and bees too were an important item. Wild animals included lion, leopard, wolf, deer, hare, wild bull, wild boar, wild goat, eagle, dove duck, snake and mouse. Daily diet consisted mainly of different sorts of bread and cakes, milk, cheese, porridge or gruel, and meat and vegetable stews. Agricultural implements have been found at various sites, and a glance through a dictionary provides words for farm, sheepfold, pig-sty, goat-pen, stable, threshing-floor, woodshed, orchard, meadow, beehive, granary, millstone, water-trough, plough, spade, cart and harness. In other words, the peasant's life was little different from that of his contemporaries anywhere in the Aegean-Middle Eastern world, and remarkably similar to that of his descendants in present-day Turkey.

The importance of agricultural production to the Hittite state can easily be seen if we consider the vast amount of food that was necessary to supply a city as big as Hattusas, not to mention the other towns of the realm. Estimates of population are notoriously inaccurate, but the capital covered an area of 414 acres, and if even half of this was occupied by houses the standard average of 150–200 persons per acre gives a figure of about 30,000–40,000 inhabitants. Since it has been calculated that the 'consumption-yield' of grain under Bronze Age agricultural conditions was about seven bushels per acre, and that annual grain-consumption under these conditions is about ten bushels per head per annum, the annual consumption of the citizens of Hattusas must have

75 Tools and agricultural implements. *Top*: chisel from Tarsus, L. 23 cm; chisel from Mersin. *Centre*: hoe from Mersin; chisel from Alaca, L. 20 cm; builder's trowel (?) from Alaca, L. 9.5 cm. *Below*: bronze hammer from Alaca, L. 12.5 cm; sickle from Tarsus, L. 26.5 cm.

been 300,000–400,000 bushels, the produce of between 40,000 and 60,000 acres of corn-land. Even if the estimated population is halved to 15,000–20,000, a figure which many regard as more realistic,[60] the acreage required for corn-production is still some 20,000–30,000. Most of the grain must have been grown in the fertile agricultural land immediately north of the city.

Trade and industry

Farming, however, was not the only livelihood available. There is evidence for the presence of doctors, builders, carpenters, stone-masons, goldsmiths, coppersmiths, potters, bakers, shoemakers, weavers, tailors, fullers, tavern-keepers (male and female), fishermen, cooks, porters and watchmen, although in many cases full-time professionals were employed only by the palace and temples. Sometimes there is evidence for what can only be described as industrial areas, especially in connection with metal-working. Smelting of ores was often (though not always) done near the mines, and recent work has shown the existence of numerous ancient mines and smelting sites.[61] Continuing research will undoubtedly yield further details, especially on the dating of such workings. In the meantime it is clear that copper ores were being mined and smelted in the northern mountains at least as early as the EB I period (dated by C^{14} to c. 2800 BC).[62] Metal was transported, probably in carts or on donkeys, and extensively traded, in the form of ingots, the best examples of which have been found not on land but in the wrecks of Late Bronze Age 76 ships, probably Syrian, off the south Turkish coast.[63] The final shaping into tools and weapons was done locally, and areas devoted to this have been found at Boğazköy and Tarsus marked by the presence of large quantities of slag. Boğazköy has also produced a fragment of a copper ingot of Cypriot type, and Tarsus part of a clay crucible with bronze still adhering to it.

76 Divers investigating a cargo of 'ox-hide' copper ingots preserved in a Late Bronze Age shipwreck off Kaş, south-west Turkey.

77 Replica of sculptured group found at Fassılar. H. 7.3 m.

Stone-carving seems to have been organized on the same lines as metalworking, with preliminary shaping being done at the quarry and the final touches being given once the statue was in position. At Yesemek, south-east of Islâhiye, literally hundreds of half-finished statues, dating to the last quarter of the second millennium and the first quarter of the first, are to be seen lying around waiting for transportation, while the colossal figure abandoned on the hillside at Fassılar, near Lake Beyşehir, may well have been on its way to its final position at the spring sanctuary of Eflatun Pınar, some 30 miles away.

An area devoted to the making of pottery has been excavated at Eskiyapar, near Alaca. In the Hittite level of this site was an open courtyard in which were situated two round kilns, each *c.* 1.5 m in diameter, with a central post and radiating struts for the floor of the upper chamber. Water was supplied through terracotta pipes, and

77

79

78 Suggested reconstruction of monument at Eflatun Pınar, near Beyşehir, with Fassılar figure top left (after Mellaart).

79 The spring sanctuary at Eflatun Pınar. The platform originally had two large figures on it, either incorporating the Fassılar statue (as shown above), or with two seated figures which were larger versions of those in relief on the lower face of the platform. The natural pool in front of the platform was enlarged in the Hittite period by a dam with a sluice.

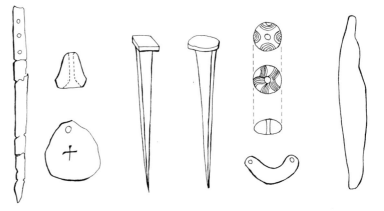

80 Knife from Troy; spindle-whorl from Kusura; loom-weight from Troy; nails from Alaca; spindle-whorl from Polatlı; loom-weight from Alaca; knife from Kusura. Not to scale.

82 (*opposite*) Steatite mould from Troy VIIa, broken at one end. On one side are the matrices for two ring-shaped pendants and three small spherical beads. On the other, four ring-pendants and three slender segmented beads. L. 8 cm.

fragments of unfired and misfired plates were recovered. Similar establishments were doubtless situated in many Hittite towns.

Other industries were more domestic in character. Spinning and weaving were done at home, as can be seen from the large numbers of spindle-whorls and loom-weights which have survived at many sites. Tailors and leather-workers, carpenters and builders, bakers and barbers, must have worked in every town and village, but evidence for their presence is more difficult to detect. That older industries also survived can be seen in a room at Kültepe which contained a large amount of worked obsidian, stored presumably for future use in such implements as threshing-sledges.

80

Clothing and jewellery

81 'Hurrian shirt' from an Egyptian relief (after Pritchard).

The normal everyday clothing for the average Hittite was a knee-length, shirt-like tunic, rather inelegantly known as the 'garment with the neck coming out'. It had long sleeves and was usually worn without a belt. A longer and more luxurious version, called a 'Hurrian shirt', was worn on festive occasions. It could be trimmed with coloured embroidery or metal decorations, and was sometimes worn with an ornamental belt or waist-band. The light tunic with a kilt, frequently to be seen on monuments, was probably military equipment for light mobile troops, and the long gown or mantle, likewise carved on the monuments, was normally worn by gods, kings and priests for religious ceremonies. Kings and priests also had round caps or head-bands, but these can be seen also on the hunters and acrobats of the Alaca reliefs. The high conical hat, a symbol of divinity, may also have been worn by the king on important state occasions. Shoes or boots with upturned toes were made in different colours and ornamented in various ways. Stockings or gaiters were also worn. The normal outdoor dress for women was a long cloak which enveloped the figure from head to foot. Beneath this was a lighter garment for use in the privacy of the house. The long pleated skirt, broad belt and high *polos*-hat of the goddesses at Yazılıkaya seem to have been reserved primarily for divinities, but the queen may sometimes have worn them in her capacity as high priestess.

Clothing was normally fastened by one or two ornamental bronze pins at the shoulders. Jewellery was worn by both sexes, and there are examples of ear-rings, finger-rings, bracelets and necklaces. Hanging pendants, probably with some sort of amuletic function, were popular – ornamental 'sun-discs', lunate shapes, pairs of shoes and animal or divine figurines, singly or in groups. Hair was usually worn long, hanging over the neck and shoulders or arranged in a pig-tail. Men were clean-shaven, and small 'cut-throat' razors have been excavated at several sites.

Seals

One particularly fine example of a finger-ring was designed to be used as a seal, but the signet-ring, like the cylinder-seal, was the exception in the Hittite world. The normal form was the stamp-seal, usually of a conical shape rising from a circular base to a ring or perforated boss by means of which it was suspended from a cord. Lens-shaped seals are also found. These have a design on each side, and are pivoted in a U-shaped metal holder for ease of use. Seals of the early Old Hittite period were a direct continuation of those of the later Colony-period. The principal motif could be purely geometric, or could take the form of an eagle, a griffin, a quadruped, a human figure, or occasionally several figures combined. Sometimes decoration was added round the border of the seal. Many of these motifs disappeared during the course of the Old Kingdom, and it was also during this period that writing was first introduced into the designs. This was in the form of 'Anatolian Hieroglyphs', which replaced the central motif within the decorated border. Among the names which can be read, those ending in -muwa and -ziti predominate, and since these are known to be Luwian in origin a strong Old Kingdom Luwian element in the population seems probable. Occasionally there is a combination of hieroglyphs with cuneiform writing.

From the time of Telepinus (*c.* 1500) onward there is an increasing number of so-called '*tabarna*-seals', first attested under Hattusilis I, and these become the characteristic royal seals of the Middle Kingdom. They consist of a small central area with ornamentation or hieroglyphs surrounded by a two-line cuneiform inscription containing the royal title *tabarna*, but almost never the name of its bearer. Parallel to these are '*tawananna*-seals' belonging to queens. On them, for some unknown reason, the central sign is in cuneiform rather than hieroglyphic Hittite.

By about 1400 royal seals were beginning to acquire the characteristics of the Imperial period. Foremost among these is the

83–4 *Left*: impression of a gold signet-ring; *above*: amuletic figurine, H. 4 cm.

aedicula, the winged sun-disc extended above the hieroglyphic name (or sometimes title) in the central area of the seals. The cuneiform legend gives the name, titles and sometimes ancestry of the monarch, and in some cases also of his queen. In the finest and most elaborate seals (first apparently in the reign of Muwatallis) the central area shows the king in the embrace of his protective deity. These seals were used in communications with foreign powers and for giving the royal assent to treaties, and represent the highest point of Hittite glyptic art. Seals of lesser mortals during the Imperial period continued the tradition of a hieroglyphic inscription within a circular border. In some cases the central inscription is accompanied by a figure – divine, human or animal – and in others the border becomes an elaborate arrangement of pictorial motifs, or even of triangular marks which seem deliberately designed to give a casual observer the impression of a royal seal with a cuneiform inscription round the edge.

Pottery: central Anatolia

Finally, some description must be given of the pottery of Late Bronze Age Anatolia. Needless to say, there was no one pottery-style prevalent over the whole area, and several different pottery-provinces can be distinguished. Pottery of 'Hittite' type was in use throughout central Anatolia and in many areas affected by Hittite political or military influence. It is predominantly monochrome, and ranges from brown through reddish-brown to red. For the most part it carries on the earlier tradition of the central area, but there is a distinct falling-off in ceramic achievement, perhaps to be associated with 'mass-production' techniques.[64] Characteristic shapes among pouring vessels are the beak-spouted jug (now slimmer and less elegant than its predecessor in the Colony period), the 'tea-pot', a jug with narrow round neck and handle from neck to shoulder, and the lentoid flask with one or three handles. Cups are rare, but bowls are found in many shapes, some with simple rounded profile and rounded rim, others with rims which show thickening on the outside or (especially in the thirteenth century) on the inside. Carinated bowls are less common, but found in all periods, and under the later Empire a plate with a wide rim is especially frequent. At this time too bowls with handles are more common than they were in earlier periods. Miniature vessels, presumably votive in purpose, are also to be found, and 'spindle-bottles' and 'libation-arms', the immediate connections of which are with north Syria and Cyprus, are indications of ceramic influence from the south-east. Characteristic of the central areas is a rare type of pottery with decoration in moulded relief. Polychrome vessels bearing ritual scenes, such as those from Bitik and Inandık, are of Old Kingdom date, and monochrome examples, known only from fragments, are to be dated to the Imperial period.

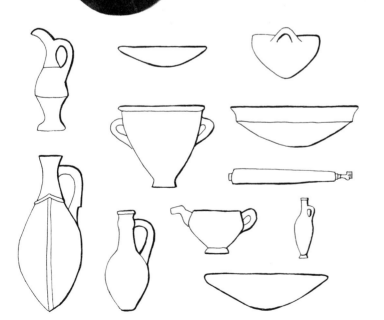

85 (*opposite*) Seal impressions. *From the top*: Old Hittite period seals, an animal and a solar motif from Boğazköy; Middle Kingdom period royal seal of Huzziyas, with double cuneiform rings and central ornamental motif; Imperial period joint royal seal, with winged sun disc above the titles of King Hattusilis III and Queen Puduhepa (see also seals of Kings Muwatallis, ill. 23; Mursilis III, ill. 24; Tudhaliyas IV, ill. 46; and Suppululiumas, ill. 41); commoners' seals: Old Kingdom seal from Boğazköy and Imperial period seal from Ugarit. Not to scale.

86 (*above left*) Vase from Inandık with relief decoration showing ritual scenes, possibly a sacred marriage. H. *c.* 1 m.

87 (*above right*) Fragment of a vessel with decoration in relief, from Bitik near Ankara. The top scene, where a man lifts a woman's veil and offers her a bowl, probably has a religious significance (a sacred marriage?). The central register shows a procession of worshippers, while below it the remains of two figures can be seen, perhaps performing a religious dance with daggers. H. of fragment 38 cm.

88 (*left*) Boğazköy; typical pottery shapes (after Fischer).

143
89
124

Perhaps the most attractive type of Hittite pottery is the vessel in the form of an animal. Lion-figures are known, but bulls are much more common, and birds, especially water-birds, also occur. The prize specimens of this type are the two large bull-vessels, each nearly 1 m tall, found in an early Imperial context on the lower part of the citadel terrace at Boğazköy. Their surfaces are coated with a highly polished red slip, and they have cream-painted patches on their foreheads, shoulders and haunches. Each also has inlaid black eyeballs, a white-painted halter attached to a nose-ring, an opening at the base of the neck to enable liquid to be poured in, and two open nostrils for pouring it out again. That the vessels were designed to form a pair can be deduced from the way their tails hang. They have been identified with Sheri and Hurri, the bulls of the Weather-god in Hurrian and Imperial Hittite cult.

Pottery of Hittite type is found as far west as the Eskişehir area. This may well represent a measure of political domination (the area has been identified with Wilusa), but the same cannot be true of northern Anatolia, although 'Hittite' pottery has been found around Kastamonu, Eflanı, Ilgaz and Gerede, as well as in the area immediately north of Hattusas at Horoztepe and at Dundartepe on the Black Sea coast near Samsun. The pottery of this area, although recognizably derivative, in some ways preserves the finer traditions of the Colony-period to a greater extent than does that of central Anatolia. Clearly the Gasga-peoples, although they tended to absorb much of Hittite culture, in some ways at least achieved a higher standard than their southern neighbours.

89 Vase in the form of a two-headed duck, from Boğazköy, H. 20.2 cm.

Another area which reflects Hittite political domination in its ceramic repertoire is Cilicia. Here too there are to be found shallow bowls or plates, lentoid flasks, narrow-necked jugs and other central Anatolian forms. In the Elazığ area also the Hittite presence can be detected in the pottery. Here grey wares which belong to an earlier local tradition are accompanied by vessels of Old Kingdom type. These are followed by characteristic Imperial forms, especially coarse plates, mostly in an orange ware as opposed to central Anatolian brown or red.

Elsewhere in eastern Anatolia ceramic evidence for the Late Bronze Age is almost non-existent. It has been suggested that after a flourishing period in the third millennium the area lapsed into nomadism for much of the second,[65] but this can only be substantiated through further research and excavation.

Pottery: western Anatolia

If we now turn to western Anatolia we move into a different ceramic world. The north-west, for instance, has its own range of shapes and fabrics, best known from Troy (late VI and VIIa), but found also down the coast as far as Smyrna, on the off-shore islands, and inland on the plains of Balıkesir and Akhisar-Manisa. The most distinctive pottery of the area is of fine quality and finished with a burnished grey slip, the 'Grey Minyan' of the publications on Troy. This is never the only pottery in use, being invariably accompanied by red or buff wares. At Troy, for instance, red ware is common in the earlier stages of level VI, but then disappears, and buff wares are characteristic of late VI and VIIa. At Smyrna, on the other hand, grey ware appears late and becomes the principal ware only in the Late Bronze Age. The pottery of the whole area, with its high handles, sharp carinations and rivet-shaped knobs, strongly suggests the existence of metallic prototypes, and it has been suggested that the grey, red and buff wares are imitations of silver, gold and copper.[66] Central Anatolian shapes such as the beak-spouted jug and the wide-rimmed plate are conspicuously lacking. Characteristic forms are bowls with straight sides, with or without a foot, carinated bowls with everted rims and often with rising handles, delicate rounded bowls, round-mouthed and trefoil-mouthed jugs, lentoid flasks, and various types of wide-mouthed jar. Decoration is largely limited to incised wavy lines, especially on the shoulders of pots, with a few raised ridges, swellings and knobs. The only exotic feature is a liking at Troy for handles in the form of animal-heads. At Troy too there is abundant evidence for the import of Mycenaean pottery and for imitation of Mycenaean shapes by local potters. Elsewhere in the area Mycenaean influence is negligible, although there are signs that imports reached as far inland as Sardis and even beyond.

The area around Iznik seems, on the evidence of surface survey, to constitute a separate pottery-province, characterized by orange-buff burnished wares with frequent pattern-burnishing, accompanied by unburnished buff vessels which may represent a simpler form of the burnished ware. Without the evidence of excavation it is difficult to date these wares with any precision.

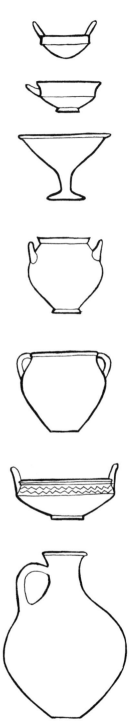

90 Typical pottery shapes of north-west Anatolia (after Blegen).

The Late Bronze Age in south-western Anatolia, best represented by levels III, II and I at Beycesultan, is marked by yet a different and distinctive type of pottery. In level III vessels with a dark brown wash survive from the Middle Bronze Age, but most pottery of this level has a polished red or buff slip. There is also a lustrous ware in red, grey or gold with a micaceous polished wash. This 'imitation metal ware' becomes by far the most popular fabric of level II, although it is still accompanied by some burnished wares. In level I many features of level II survive, but these are gradually replaced by a new slipped ware in a range of distinctive colours – off-white, orange, pink, plum-red and others – and by a coarse kitchen-ware decorated with rope-impressions.

91–2 The most characteristic south-western shapes are a variety of chalices and 'fruit-stands', one-handled 'beer-mugs', carinated bowls, usually without handles, flat-rimmed plates, bifoil- and trefoil-mouthed jugs, jugs with elongated 'bearded' beak-spouts, and large and small *askoi* which must reflect Aegean influence. A curious vessel peculiar to level II is the 'drink-warmer', a two-handled vessel divided horizontally into two compartments. The upper of these is bowl-shaped, while the lower is provided with an opening through which charcoal could be inserted and with ventilation-holes to provide a draught. No contemporary parallels for these vessels are known.

The Late Bronze Age ceramic material in the south-west forms a fairly homogeneous whole until the introduction in level I of foreign features, most of which seem to have their origin in central Anatolia.

91 Pottery from Level II, Beycesultan.

These were at first taken to be signs of a refugee element which arrived in the south-west after the destruction of the Hittite Empire, but a detailed ceramic comparison suggests that the central features at Beycesultan are to be dated to the thirteenth rather than the twelfth century. No convincing historical reason for their appearance at that time has so far been suggested.

Some scholars, it should be added here, have suggested that the Late Bronze Age material from Beycesultan has so many parallels in the central Anatolian Middle Bronze Age that it should in fact be dated to that period rather than to the later second millennium. But the occurrence of micaceous wares (though not of chalices) at Aphrodisias in conjunction with local imitations of Mycenaean pottery[67] is a strong pointer towards the later period. The final publication of the material should help to resolve this problem.[68]

92 Beycesultan: typical pottery shapes (after Mellaart).

Mycenaean pottery in Anatolia

The discovery of Mycenaean pottery around the coast of Anatolia raises again the question of possible contacts between the Anatolian and Aegean worlds. For the most part it seems clear that such contacts were confined to coastal trading by Mycenaean merchants, and that inland penetration was minimal. Excavations of settlements and graveyards at Miletus, Iasos and Müsgebi, however, have left little doubt that there was genuine Mycenaean occupation on the southern part of the west coast. This has been taken by some to be sufficient reason for locating a Mycenaean kingdom, known to the Hittites as Millawanda, in this area. But as we have seen in chapter 3, it is difficult

93 Mycenaean IIIB flask
from Maşat H. 10 cm.

to accept this location for Millawanda without creating other geographical and historical problems, and the question must for the moment be left open. One can only say that although Mycenaean contact with the Hittites along the west coast remains problematical, contact with Arzawa, though not yet recognizable in the available evidence, is in geographical terms much more likely.

Some sort of direct Hittite-Mycenaean contact is suggested by the discovery of Mycenaean IIIB vessels at Maşat Hüyük in central Anatolia, well away from any coast. But the form which that contact took has yet to be satisfactorily explained. Since fragments of Mycenaean pottery occur in several different buildings, the vessels can scarcely have been 'souvenirs' brought home by some far-travelling citizen, yet their numbers are not sufficient to suggest an active trade between Maşat and the Aegean world, either via the Black Sea or via Cilicia. Had such trade existed, one would have expected signs of it also at Hattusas, where Mycenaean imports are conspicuously lacking. Future discoveries at Maşat or elsewhere may, in the end, offer some enlightenment.

7
Religion

The religious beliefs and practices of a community can seldom be tidily arranged as a unified system. Often the patterns of action and belief have built up over centuries – even over millennia – with alterations and additions as outside influences enter or social and economic conditions change, until the result seems to the outsider a self-contradictory hotch-potch of meaningless ritual and largely identical deities. Hittite religion is a good example of this confusion. Its roots reach back to the Neolithic period, and numerous additions and alterations between the sixth millennium and the second result in a complicated amalgam which the Hittite theologians themselves had great difficulty in organizing into an 'official' cult and pantheon. Behind this state organization we may be able to trace many of the diverse elements, native and imported, which were partially fused to form the Imperial system.

The Anatolian background

The oldest religion of Anatolia, like that of many other parts of the world, may be seen to have been primarily concerned with the relationship of mankind to the great powers of nature. Of these the most important was undoubtedly the life-giving earth, the mother of all

94 'Mother-goddess' figure from Çatal Hüyük. The head is restored.

95 Statuette of a seated goddess, thirteenth or fourteenth century BC. From Alaca Hüyük. H. 6.6 cm.

things. A lesser position was held by her consort, a deity connected with the fertilizing power of water, without whose help the earth-mother could not conceive. These powers, and many others, were essential for the well-being and continuity of life, and it was necessary both for the individual and for the community to gain and keep their favour by the regular performance of appropriate ritual actions. So each village had its own protective deities, cult-centre, mythology and festival calendar linked mainly to the agricultural year. In each village too there were witches or medicine-men, who would enact rituals to counter specific disasters or achieve specific aims.

This simple (and it must be admitted hypothetical) picture became complicated as soon as political unity began to be established on a larger scale than that of the agricultural village. When communities combined, there is little sign that one group of deities replaced another, or that basically similar deities were recognized as one. The separate identity of local divinities was preserved, and the result was a pantheon of increasing size and complexity. Some gods and goddesses emerged as more powerful than others, but the worship of the less powerful continued on the age-old pattern. For the most part these deities are now little more than names to us, but some of them were to become the principal figures of the Hittite pantheon.

The earliest element that we can with any confidence detect in Hittite religious and other texts is the Hattian one. To this people belong such deities as the 'Sun-goddess' (rather an underworld goddess) of Arinna, the 'Weather-god' (rather a water-god) Taru, the 'Sun-deity' Estan, the 'War-god' Wurunkatte, the 'Throne-goddess' Halmasuit, the 'Genius of Hattusas' Inara, the 'disappearing god' Telepinu, and a dozen or so more of lesser importance. These deities were survivors of a native, pre-Hittite pantheon which formed the basis of the second-millennium religious system.

The non-Anatolian background

Non-Anatolian peoples too played a part in the formation of Hittite religion. Of these peoples the most important were the Indo-European-speakers who arrived in central Anatolia in the latter part of the third millennium, and the Hurrians whose influence can be increasingly seen during the course of the second. It is in fact surprisingly difficult to find anything Indo-European in the Imperial religious system. The newcomers may well have brought their Zeus with them, and his influence has been seen in some of the attributes of the thunder-wielding god of the mountain-tops who is the consort of the Mother Goddess in the official pantheon.[69] Other Indo-European features have been inferred from the iconography of the Karum II period (c. 1940–1840) at Kültepe as seen on the impressions of cylinder-seals found there. In previous centuries, if one can judge from statues and figurines, the Mother Goddess had been supreme, but on the seal-impressions we find a pantheon which is predominantly male, with the Weather-god paramount and an important position given to Pirwa, a god whose close links with the horse have suggested to some a connection with horse-using Indo-European invaders. But if foreign

96

gods achieved a temporary dominance during the Colony-period, it is clear that the Mother Goddess fairly quickly regained her position of primacy. The Hittite Weather-god, though a powerful deity, is very decidedly subordinate to the leading lady in the pantheon.

Hurrian influence in Hittite religion is far stronger and more widespread. It has been suggested that the dynasty of the Imperial period, beginning probably about 1430 with the accession of Tudhaliyas I and his queen Nikalmati, was Hurrian in origin, and by the time of Suppiluliumas the process of Hurrianization was gathering speed. In the thirteenth century, largely because of the influence of Puduhepa, the Hurrian wife of Hattusilis III, there was a virtual 'take-over' of official religion, and so by the end of the century the pantheon was fully Hurrianized. This can be seen most clearly in the sculptures of the open-air sanctuary at Yazılıkaya, where the assembled deities of the Hittite pantheon are arranged in Hurrian order and given names that are linguistically Hurrian. Here the principal deities, earlier known as the Weather-god of Hatti and the Sun-goddess of Arinna, are named Teshub and Hebat, and are accompanied by their children Alanzu and Sharruma, and by deities with such names as Kumarbi, Sausga, Nikkal and many more. It must be stressed that syncretism of this type is late and untypical.

96 Impression of a cylinder-seal from Kültepe, showing the god Pirwa standing on a four-wheeled chariot drawn by four horses. Facing him is the god Adad standing on a lion–dragon and holding a spear and a thunderbolt. A human figure lies prostrate under the chariot.

113, 114

Village religion

The religion of the Hittite Empire is thus the end-product of a long and complicated process.[70] Most of the surviving evidence relates to the official state-cult, but one can also catch glimpses of the religious activities of the smaller communities of the Anatolian plateau. Little is known of local religious buildings, but inventories of their contents, preserved at the capital, tell us something of their furnishings and their festivals. The principal object in a shrine was a cult-image of modest size, usually a weapon, an animal or a *huwasi*-stone, an upright stela set on a carved base. Only towards the end of the Imperial period were these objects beginning to be replaced by anthropomorphic images, usually the gift of the king. The principal festivals took place in the

105

97 (*opposite*) Rock relief at
Sirkeli near Adana, with
figure of Muwatallis.

spring and autumn, and in many cases involved the carrying of the
image of the god to a *huwasi*-stone set up in a walled-off sacred area
somewhere in the open country outside the community. Sacrifice was
followed by a communal meal, and then by mock-battles or sporting
contests, after which the image was returned to the shrine.

Other activities, which we would tend to describe as being 'magic'
rather than 'religious', were also a feature of everyday life in both
country and town. Sickness and misfortune, whether due to the anger
of the gods or the evil activities of hostile men, were a constant hazard,
and to counteract such things elaborate rituals, making much use of
'sympathetic magic', were evolved for every purpose from averting
impotence to persuading a reluctant deity to return to his shrine. Local
priests, often called 'diviners' or 'bird-operators', and priestesses
known as 'old women' were in charge of such ceremonies, and much of
the action took place in the suppliant's house or in the open air. In this
connection springs as sources of underground water were especially
important. Traces of simple 'sacred springs' do not often survive, but a
rock-monument like Eflatun Pınar, marking as it does a perennial
spring, may well be an elaborated version of a common type of open-air
shrine. Other rock-monuments, such as that of Muwatallis at Sirkeli
and the much-worn 'Niobe' figure (now thought to be male) at Sipylus,
are clearly positioned above flowing water, and these too may be
connected with similar beliefs. A possible spring-shrine on a less
pretentious scale has been discovered near Ilgın, where a spring at the
foot of a hill was provided with a rectangular stone basin, whose walls
were inscribed with a long hieroglyphic inscription which includes the
cartouche of Tudhaliyas IV.

Small buildings used for cult purposes also existed in Hattusas itself,
and several have recently been excavated in the southern part of the
city. A simple three-roomed structure in the residential part of the
lower town is also probably typical of the many small shrines, served by
a single priest, which existed both here and all over the country. Some
buildings on the citadel also seem to be connected with domestic cult,
and these too may eventually find parallels at other sites. Building C of
the late Imperial period had five rooms grouped around a central open
area, whose floor was sunk 1.5 m below those of the surrounding rooms.
On the floor were layers of mud and sand in which were numerous nests
of shells and votive vessels, and there was an outlet for water in one
corner. An earlier building (level IVb2) on the lower terrace of the
citadel seems also to have had a central area with a drain and a sunken
floor, on which lay a large painted vase in the form of a duck. Again a
connection with water seems probable.

In western Asia Minor we are lucky enough to have at Beycesultan a
number of late Bronze Age shrines which were found in a trench which
was opened in an effort to locate the city wall. These consist of pairs of
long narrow rooms, each *c*. 9 m by 3 m, with entrances at one short end
and smaller rooms (labelled 'sacristies' by the excavators) at the other.
Towards the sacristy end of each shrine was a low platform on which
stood a pair of terracotta 'horns' backed by a low wall. The horns
themselves were decorated all over with a stamped ornament in the
form of concentric circles, and in one case a cooking-pot stood on a

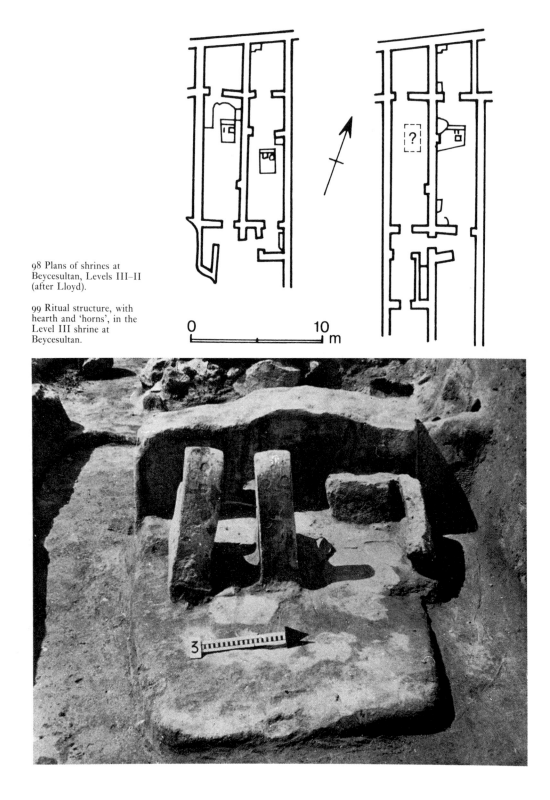

98 Plans of shrines at
Beycesultan, Levels III–II
(after Lloyd).

99 Ritual structure, with
hearth and 'horns', in the
Level III shrine at
Beycesultan.

0   10
                        m

100 Ritual structure, with hearth and 'horns', in the Level II shrine at Beycesultan.

small clay pillar to the right of the horns. The remains of a similar structure were found in a contemporary house in another part of the settlement, and yet another example has been excavated at Kusura. In the latter instances there is not much to suggest that these structures were anything other than domestic hearths, but it is difficult to see the best-preserved horns from Beycesultan as mere 'pot-holders', and the quantity of pottery, bead necklaces and bronze implements and weapons preserved in the rooms does not suggest ordinary domestic occupation.

State religion: the king

If we turn now to the more imposing religious structures of Boğazköy, we are immediately brought face to face with some of the most impressive monuments of Hittite imperialism. With the rise of Hittite power deities who had originally been the protectors of small agricultural communities fairly quickly found themselves the guardians of a royal house and an extensive empire. But their basic nature, and their relation to man, did not change. In Hittite eyes the gods were the masters, and the purpose of man was to serve god as a good servant does his master. In return the god, like a good master, provided protection from sickness, famine and enemy action, and punished any bad servant who had neglected his ritual duty. So in effect, as Hittite power grew, an ever-increasing burden was placed on the shoulders of the king. As the gods' principal servant he was responsible for tending all the deities of his realms, and thus became a key figure in binding the empire into a single unified structure. His primary duty was that of ensuring the favour of the gods by an annual round of visits to their shrines at the seasons appropriate to their festivals, and by what at times seems an obsessive concern with the purity of his own person and actions. If he failed in any way to perform his duties, the gods were angry, and it was his responsibility to find the cause of their anger, to make amends, and to request forgiveness. In such a situation it was difficult to discover what precise offence had been committed, for although the gods were conceived in human terms they did not make themselves immediately manifest to a worshipper in bodily form in order to tell him the nature of his offence. Occasionally they would speak through the mouth of an ecstatic, more frequently they would pass on a message in a dream; but normally the nature of the offence had to be discovered by resort to divination – by examination of the entrails of sacrificial victims, by noting the flight of birds, or by means of a type of lottery of which the details remain obscure. The procedure was to ask, 'Is such-and-such the cause of god's anger?', and to go on listing possible offences until the omens gave a favourable answer. When the reason for the deity's wrath was discovered the suppliant could speak directly to his god in prayer, and it is in their prayers that we can most clearly see Hittite kings (and queens and princes) as human beings struggling with human problems and seeking answers to them. The 'plague prayers' of Mursilis II are perhaps the finest example of a Hittite monarch burdened by a sense of personal responsibility for a disaster which afflicts the state.

Boğazköy: the Great Temple

For the most part, however, the duties of a monarch were concerned with public ritual rather than private prayer, and the performance of his duties by a Great King demanded an appropriate setting. This setting was provided by a huge temple-complex (Temple I) set in a prominent position in the lower city. It formed a roughly square area of *c.* 275 m a side, surrounded by a temenos-wall which was partly the old wall of the lower city, but was for the most part specially built for the purpose. The temple-buildings themselves stood roughly in the centre of this area. The ground to the west and north-west (i.e. *behind* the temple from the point of view of the monarch resident in the citadel to the south-east) was occupied by the houses of the numerous temple personnel. These varied in size. Some were terraced down the slope of the hill along main roads with a number of smaller streets and alleyways separating them into blocks. Others, especially in the northern part of the precinct, were free-standing, and presumably belonged to functionaries of higher rank. The approach to this residential area from the lower part of the town was by means of a monumental gateway in the middle of the north-western wall. On the opposite side there must have been a ceremonial entrance for the king in the immediate area of the Scribal School,[71] a large two-storeyed building which stood immediately beside the temenos-wall to the south-east, alongside the only practicable route down from the citadel to the temple buildings. Between this gate and the buildings themselves the ground was completely open, offering an uninterrupted view of the temple

102–3
103

101 View of the main temple-complex at Boğazköy, seen from Büyükkaya

102 Outline plan of the main temple-complex at Boğazköy. A, section of old city-wall; B, temenos-wall; C, temple-buildings; D, houses; E, gate from lower city; F, open space; G, Scribal School; H, main gate (?); J, postern-tunnel.

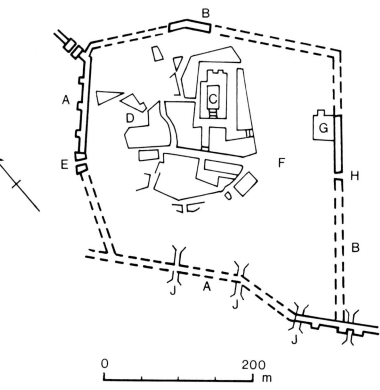

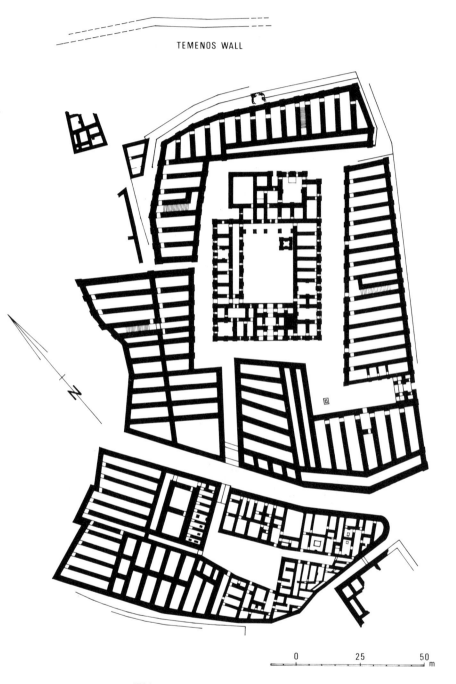

TEMENOS WALL

0   25   50
                  m

103 Detail-plan of Temple I
at Boğazköy (after Bittel).

structure. This was supported on a massive artificial terrace, *c.* 137 m
long by 100 m wide, which on its western side cut through earlier
domestic buildings and thus represents a thirteenth-century expansion
of the temple. Round the edge of this terrace were ranges of long
narrow store-rooms supporting an upper storey and forming an almost

totally enclosed paved area in which stood the temple itself. The principal gateway to this area was near the south-east corner, opposite the Scribal School, but there were three other entrances to the north-east, north-west, and south-west.

The temple-building proper was entered by an elaborate gateway designed in the characteristic Hittite manner – a central gate-room with porters' lodges to right and left, and both inside and outside this a vestibule with small rooms on either side which had large windows opening on to the outer paved area or the inner court. In a corner at the opposite end of the courtyard stood a small building used for ritual ablutions, and behind this a colonnade fronted the entrance to the innermost part of the temple, a structure built in granite rather than the limestone used for the rest of the complex. Here were situated the shrines of the deities of the temple – in this case presumably the Weather-god of Hatti and the Sun-goddess of Arinna – where the divine images stood on low platforms of stone. No cult-statue has survived, but it can be seen from the size of surviving bases that they must have been life-sized, and we can assume that, like the images in smaller shrines, they were made from, or adorned with, precious metals. In many ways they must have resembled the figures carved in low relief on such monuments as Yazılıkaya. Occasionally a deity, especially the Weather-god, would be represented by his sacred animal, as can be seen on a relief from Alaca Hüyük, or by a weapon such as a sword or spear.

104

115–21

137

It has often been pointed out that the innermost shrines of Hittite temples were not immediately accessible, or even visible, from the courtyard. Whatever went on in them was the business of a select few, and the image of the deity was kept out of sight of worshippers gathered outside. It is also worth noting that the cult-rooms, and indeed most of

104 The entrance to the main building of Temple I. Note the low sills of the large windows on either side of the doorway.

105 A stone pedestal with a scene on the side showing a worshipper before a similar base topped by an upright stele. This is probably the cult-object referred to in the texts as a *huwasi*-stone, and a similar object may well have stood on the pedestal itself. H. 92.5 cm.

the rooms of the temple, received light not from the inner courtyard but from windows in the outside walls. The building was thus integrated with the outer parts of the complex rather than shut off from it.

Inside the temple area many of the great festivals of the Hittite calendar must have taken place. These consisted largely of ritual washings, sacrifices and libations in different parts of the shrine. Cult equipment included sun- and moon-discs, vessels of precious metals, 124, 143 and pottery rhyta, often in the form of bulls and other animals. Not only the cult-statue, but also the royal throne and parts of the temple-building itself were regarded as sacred, and *huwasi*-stones, upright 105 stelae set in a special carved base, also had an important part to play. 'Great Assemblies', presumably in the courtyards, were a frequent occurrence, and there were constant processions by the king and his bodyguard, priests, dignitaries, and temple-servants, often accompanied by singers and musicians playing several types of instrument.

The temple was not merely the building in which the great festivals took place, but also the home of the god throughout the year. In it he had his dining-room and his bedroom, and he had at his command a host of temple-servants to attend to his every need. Some at least of these servants presumably occupied the houses at the rear of the temple-precinct, but others lived in the residential part of the town and 103 others again may have lived and worked in a curious, irregularly shaped complex *c.* 120 m long and 55 m wide, situated immediately south-west of the main temple buildings, separated from them by a 7.5 m-wide paved road, and entered by a single gateway immediately opposite one of the subsidiary temple-entrances. The gateway leads to a trapezoidal courtyard nearly 30.5 m long with a maximum width of *c.* 15 m.

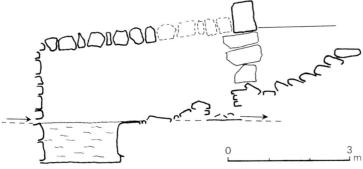

106 The entrance to the underground pool in the main temple-complex at Boğazköy. The right-hand part of the broken lintel, seen restored to its original position, has the figure of a worshipper incised on it.

107 Section of the underground pool structure shown above (after Bittel).

Surrounding this courtyard, and opening off it, or off alleyways or corridors leading from it, are sixteen independent units of different sizes. Here may well have been situated the kitchens, breweries, workshops, equipment-stores and scribal chambers of the temple. The whole complex has been compared to similar Egyptian workers' compounds at Amarna and Deir-el-Medineh.

There are other building-complexes, besides those already mentioned, within the area of the temple-precinct, but they are for the most part still imperfectly known. A large rectangular building (Complex 2), comparable in many ways to the buildings in the citadel, lay immediately south of the workers' compound, and behind it, in an open square, was a small subterranean pool covered by a low corbel-vault and entered from the north by a flight of stone steps. Water entered the pool through a hole in the back wall, and was carried off under the steps to a channel beneath the road outside. Over the entry to this grotto was an incised group of figures of which only one survives,

106–7

with traces of a second. The intact figure is that of a man facing left, wearing a long robe and a round cap, and raising his arm in the conventional gesture of adoration. Everything points to a non-secular use for this structure which once again lays emphasis on the divine connections of spring-water.

Boğazköy: other temples

Four other temples have been known for many years, all of them skilfully sited on natural plateaux in the high southern part of the city and looking down over the lower town. Despite differences of detail they correspond closely in plan to Temple I. Each has a ceremonial entrance, a central courtyard with colonnade, and an offset inner sanctuary with windows opening to the outside rather than to the court. Temples II, III and IV have one cult-room each. Temple V, like Temple I, has two, but in this case, for some unknown reason, one of the two was built to one side of the courtyard rather than at the end of it.

In recent years excavation in the upper city has revealed two further temples (Temples VI and VII) and ten smaller buildings which contained large quantities of pottery of votive type and showed in their plans a close similarity to the larger temples. It now looks as though the entire southern part of the upper city was by the time of Tudhaliyas IV, to whom these building-works can be ascribed, a sacred area used solely for temples and shrines. The deities to whom the various buildings were dedicated cannot be identified, but presumably the temples belonged to major figures in the Hittite pantheon. The smaller ones

108

109–11

108 Plans of Temples II–V, Boğazköy (after Bittel).

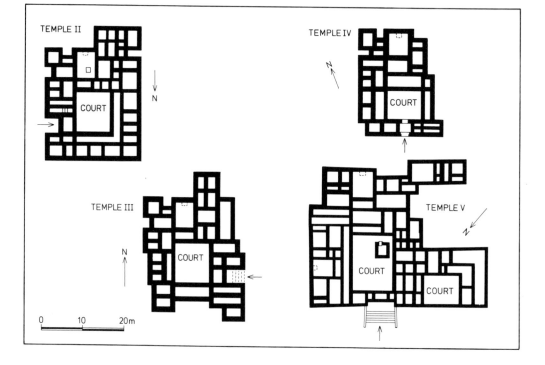

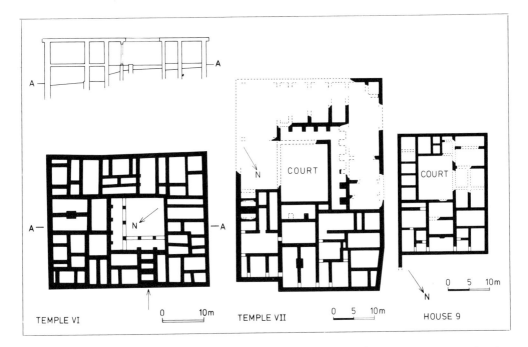

TEMPLE VI   0   10m   TEMPLE VII   0 5 10m   HOUSE 9

may have been the shrines of lesser gods and goddesses, and one is reminded of the fact, known from the texts, that many deities whose main residences were in towns other than Hattusas also had establishments in the capital which could be visited by the king as chief priest without making it necessary for him to involve himself in a series of long journeys. Further investigation may well reveal more such buildings in future years.

109–11 *Left*: plan and section of Temple VI, Boğazköy; *centre*: plan of Temple VII, Boğazköy. *Right*: plan of 'House 9', Boğazköy; there is a clear similarity to the standard temple-plan. (After Neve).

Yazılıkaya

About three-quarters of a mile north-east of Boğazköy lies Yazılıkaya, the most impressive of all Hittite religious structures. Here, at a point where a spring of fresh water once flowed, is an outcrop of rock which forms two natural chambers of different sizes. The site is in many respects like other Anatolian spring-sanctuaries, and may well have been a place of worship for hundreds of years before the rise of Hittite power. The first stage in its elaboration was the building, perhaps about 1500 BC, of an irregular wall which shut off the main chamber from the outside world. Under Hattusilis III this was replaced by a temple-complex with a strong resemblance to the temples of the capital. A large gate-building contained a staircase which led through a second gate into a rectangular courtyard containing an altar and a detached lustration-room. A pillared gateway to the left then led into the principal chamber, which took the place of the inner cult-rooms of the city buildings. A second gatehouse beyond the courtyard and its subsidiary rooms at first gave access to the smaller chamber, but after a fire in the temple during the reign of Tudhaliyas IV the rooms at the back of the courtyard were rebuilt and turned towards an entrance

113

112

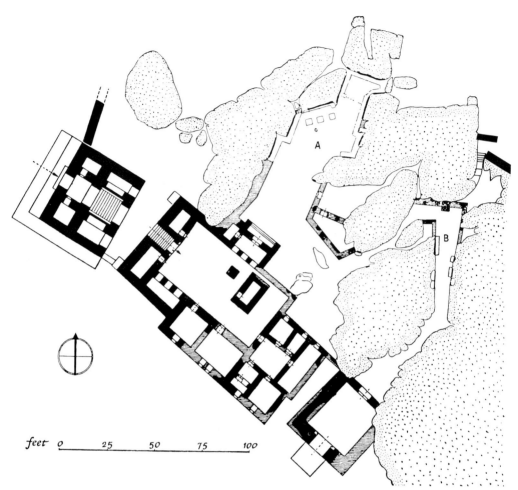

112 Plan of Yazılıkaya (after Akurgal).

which led from the larger into the smaller chamber; the whole complex was converted into a single unit.

The principal interest of Yazılıkaya however lies not in the temple buildings but in the figures carved in low relief on the rock walls of the 114–17 two natural chambers. Those in the larger one (Chamber A) give the impression of two processions, one of male and one of female deities, advancing on either side towards the rear wall, where the principal god and goddess, emphasized both by their positions and by their greater size, confront one another at the focal point of the chamber. Near the rear of the right-hand procession is the figure of a Hittite king, again on a larger scale, identified by his accompanying cartouche as a 117 Tudhaliyas. Behind him a narrow passage, guarded at its entrance by a pair of demons with wings and lion-heads, leads to the smaller chamber (Chamber B), a smooth-walled cleft no more than 2.7 m wide with a subsidiary chamber, some 9 m deep, opening off its north-eastern corner. At the back of this subsidiary chamber a wall of cyclopean masonry shuts it off from the outside world except at the left-hand end, where a narrow staircase provided an entry, possibly for the priest in

charge of whatever went on in this holy-of-holies. In front of the wall is a smoothed limestone base, and the fill around it proved on excavation to contain a great deal of wood ash. On the wall of Chamber B, next to the entry to the subsidiary chamber and clearly connected with it, is another Tudhaliyas cartouche, and further down the same wall is the most arresting and tantalizing sculpture of all. It represents an enormous sword, apparently driven into the rock, for the lower part of the blade is not represented. The hilt of the sword consists of two lions hanging head downwards, surmounted by the foreparts of two more lions facing right and left, and then by a human head facing towards the subsidiary chamber and shown by its high pointed hat to be that of a deity. Behind this great carving, *c.* 3.3 m high, is a smaller group of two figures. The larger, identified as the god Sharruma, embraces the smaller (a Tudhaliyas again) in a protective gesture. On the opposite wall, and again facing towards the subsidiary chamber, is a group of twelve soldier-like deities (who also appear at the rear of the male procession in the outer chamber) moving menacingly at a fast trot with their sickle-swords at the slope across their shoulders.

113 A view of Yazılıkaya from the south-east, showing the remains of the temple buildings and the outer part of Chamber A.

119

120

121

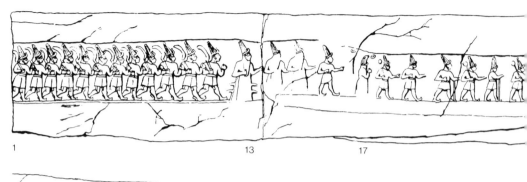

1   13   17

40   46

114 The rock-reliefs in Chamber A at Yazılıkaya (after Garstang).

115 Chamber A at Yazılıkaya, showing the rear part of the procession of male deities.

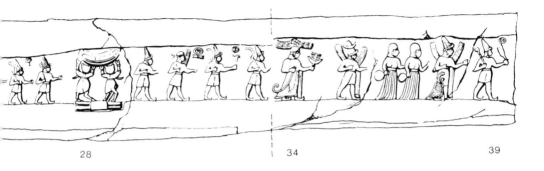

28   34   39

49   55   63

116 The central group of figures in Chamber A at Yazılıkaya.

117 The figure of King Tudhaliyas, which stands at the rear of the female procession in Chamber A at Yazılıkaya.

The problems of interpreting the sculptures of Yazılıkaya in terms of ritual and belief have certainly not all been solved. It has been pointed out by the excavator that the temple buildings, unlike those of the capital, were flimsily constructed and cannot have supported an upper storey. This suggests to him that they were not in daily use, but were reserved for some special function, perhaps an annual event.[72] This event, he plausibly suggests, was the great spring festival, held at the beginning of each new year, lasting over a month, attended by all the gods, and perhaps culminating in a 'sacred marriage' of the type so diligently documented by Sir James Frazer.

This interpretation, well as it fits the larger chamber, cannot be applied to the smaller, which must have had a different purpose. Any attempt to discover this purpose must take into account the private nature of this inner 'chapel' and the significance of the huge sculpture portraying the sword in the rock. The nearest parallel to this curious weapon dates from the Colony period and is dedicated to the god of the

118 A view of Chamber B at Yazılıkaya, showing the narrowness of the chamber and the great size of the sculptures in it.

underworld. A Hittite ritual text dealing with gods resident in the underworld describes how a priest makes images of them in the shape of swords and fixes them into the ground. Moreover, in another text the god of the underworld is connected with 'the twelve gods of the cross-roads' (whoever they may be), and one is reminded of the twelve running gods on the western wall. To all this must be added the fact that burials were found in the rocks surrounding the chamber, and that sometimes these included bird as well as human skeletons. In one case for instance a bird had been pinned down in position by fourteen large nails. Since birds are known from texts to have been sacrificed to the deities of the underworld, the excavator's conclusion that the inner chamber is a mortuary chapel of some kind is almost irrefutable.[73] The connection with Tudhaliyas (presumably the fourth of that name, since he is known to have regarded Sharruma as his protective deity) suggests that it was dedicated either to that monarch after his death or by him to some ancestor, probably an earlier namesake. A statue of the monarch

120

119 (*opposite*) The 'sword god' in Chamber B at Yazılıkaya.

120 Tudhaliyas in the embrace of his protective deity. Chamber B at Yazılıkaya.

121 The 'soldier-gods' in Chamber B at Yazılıkaya.

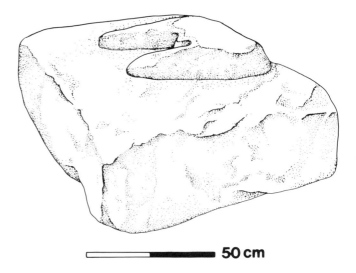

122 Fragment of a colossal basalt statue. Yekbaz, near Boğazköy.

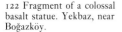

50 cm

probably stood on the stone platform at the northern end of the chamber, and what may well be a fragment of it has been found in a nearby village, ingloriously functioning as a domestic wash-board.[74]

122 The fragment still shows the slippered feet of a figure which must originally, if carved to scale, have stood some 3.5 m high. It is just possible to see that it was clad in an ankle-length robe. It may then have been a three-dimensional representation of the king as he is portrayed elsewhere in the complex. It can also be suggested that the ashes of the dead king were deposited in one of the small rectangular recesses which have been cut into the walls of the chamber. If this was so, all trace of them has long since disappeared.

Burial-practices

This conclusion leads us to the subject of burial-practices. Evidence for these again comes from both textual and archaeological sources. Several graveyards dating from the Old Hittite period are now known: Osmankayası between Boğazköy and Yazılıkaya; Ilıca some forty miles west of Ankara; Gordion the later Phrygian capital; Büget north of Çorum; Seydiler and Yanarlar, both near Afyon; Kazankaya near Maşat. Known cemeteries of the Hittite Empire period are much rarer. In all cases the burials are those of ordinary people. Royal tombs laden with gold, such as are to be found in contemporary kingdoms like Egypt and Mycenae, have not been discovered in Anatolia. The only possible exception to this is the structure known as Gavurkalesi, south-west of Ankara, where a terraced processional way leads to a hill-top plateau, some 36.5 m square, fortified by walls of cyclopean masonry. At the head of the ascent a natural rock-face bears a carved relief showing two

15 gods advancing to confront a seated goddess, while at the rear of the plateau lies a burial chamber, long since robbed, measuring *c.* 4 m by 3 m. This could well be the type of grave in which we know from textual evidence that the remains of monarchs were deposited.

Hittite kings were cremated, and comparisons have often been made between their funerals and those of the heroes of the Homeric poems.[75] Since until fairly recently no tradition of cremation was known to exist in either the Mycenaean or the Hittite world, and since a graveyard at Troy, dated to the latest phase of Troy VI, consists entirely of cremation burials, the argument was that both the Homeric and the Hittite rituals were adopted through contact with north-west Anatolia. More recent evidence suggests that this is an over-simplification. Cremation is now known to have been practised in Greece as early as the Middle Bronze Age,[76] and to have been widespread in central Anatolia from the very beginning of the Hittite period. The excavation of a large number of cremation-graves at Gedikli, in the plain of Islâhiye in south-eastern Turkey, which are clearly dated to the E.B. III period (i.e. the latter part of the third millennium) gives a pointer to the direction from which the practice may have come, and the presence of vessels of the type Schliemann termed *depas amphikypellon* in the Gedikli graves shows a clear connection with Troy II, although the nature of this connection is not yet fully understood. Cremation-graves in Greece, such as those in the cemetery at Perati, also point to connections with the Levantine area.

There are now many examples of cremation-burial in Late Bronze Age Anatolia, and the cemetery at Troy is only one of several known and excavated. The graves there lay on the southern edge of the plateau *c.* 500 m south of the citadel. The ashes of the dead were placed in jars of different shapes and sizes, which were covered with a lid and stood upright in shallow graves, often only a few centimetres below the surface of the ground. Funeral gifts were few in number and of no great intrinsic value – beads, small pottery vessels and a few pins and rings of bronze. There is no sign that graves were individually marked, or that

123 The 'crematory' at Troy VI. The spaces between the three brick piers may have been stoke-holes or air-vents for a furnace in which bodies were burned.

123   the graveyard had any sort of boundary-marking. A walled enclosure below the western foot of the citadel showed abundant traces of burning in association with the remains of human bones, and another mud-brick structure, *c.* 200 m north-west of the cemetery, may have been a furnace. This is reminiscent of the earlier graveyard at Gedikli, where there were also hearths for the burning of the dead in the area where they were finally laid to rest.

The cemetery at Boğazköy also lies outside the city, beside the road which leads to the Yazılıkaya shrine. Here large numbers of burials, some cremations and others simple inhumations, were tucked into niches and crevices in the natural rock. Stratigraphically the graves cover a period from the eighteenth to the fourteenth century. Again the remains were deposited in pottery vessels of different shapes and sizes, many of which, like those at Troy, were already broken when they were used as funerary urns. This may be a sign of poverty, or it may have some ritual significance. Grave-gifts were restricted to shells, small pots, some bronze wire, and one stamp-seal. Many graves are distinguished by the presence of animal remains. The bones of cattle, sheep and pigs presumably represent the remains of some sort of funeral feast; dog-bones tend to be taken as evidence for man's desire for faithful companionship in the other world, but there is textual evidence for dog-sacrifice with magical or ritual associations. The remains of horses (two skulls and a number of fragments) may be significant in showing some sort of ultimate connection with the practice of the nomadic pastoralists of the Russian steppe, and thus providing a tenuous link with the *Kurgan*-peoples who are thought to have introduced Indo-European languages to Anatolia. The presence of eleven donkey-skulls and other bone-fragments suggests that some inhabitants of Hattusas could not afford a sacrificial horse and had to make do with a cheaper alternative.

One disturbing feature of the cemetery was that a high proportion of the burials which survived intact contained the remains of an adult and a child buried together. This may be nothing more than coincidence, but the possibility of some sort of child-sacrifice cannot be excluded.

The graveyard at Ilıca, which can be dated to the Old Hittite period, also consists of mixed cremations and inhumations, but with the former predominating. Here the remains were deposited in damaged beak-spouted vessels and buried with the spouts facing east. Again there are animal bones, and grave-gifts are few. What distinguished this site is the presence of megalithic grave-markers, or rather row-markers, for they do not serve to distinguish individual graves. These are arranged to form one or two lines *c.* 200 m long. Originally there may have been far more of them, and in fact markers may have been typical of many contemporary cemeteries, though in most cases they have long ago been removed.

Ilıca lies only about 40 miles from Gordion, so it is surprising to find that the cemetery at that site, which is in part contemporary with Ilıca, contains no known cremation-burials at all, but consists entirely of inhumations, some in simple earth-graves, some in cist-graves, but the great majority in *pithoi*. It is probable that the simple inhumations were the earliest (dated to the Colony period), and that by the Old Hittite period most if not all the burials were in *pithos*-graves. Skeletons in the *pithoi* were buried in a contracted position with the head towards the south-east. The lack of cremations may represent a genuine difference in local burial-habits, but more probably it means that cremation-graves exist at Gordion but have yet to be found. The burials at Seydiler and Yanarlar were also in *pithoi*, and may be compared with those at Gordion. At Kazankaya bodies were deposited in pits which were then covered with stones and broken pottery. At Büget some burials were in *pithoi*, others in stone cists. The impression one gains is that *pithos*-burial was the prevalent tradition towards the west. In central Anatolia the tradition was not so strong, and alternative methods of burial were sometimes acceptable.

Despite the use of extra-mural cemeteries, it is clear that intra-mural inhumation was also fairly common. At Boğazköy, for instance, bodies were often buried in or near the houses. Most were placed in simple earth-graves, but there were departures from this – burial under stone slabs, and in one case disposal under the two halves of a *pithos* cut lengthwise. Grave-gifts in intra-mural burials were also few in number and poor in quality. All burials in and round the city seem to be those of ordinary citizens, and no social distinctions can be made in terms of type or location of burial.

124 Pair of ritual bull-vases
from Boğazköy. H. 91 cm.

Art and literature

Hittite art

The immediate reaction of anyone who turns to the art of Anatolia between 1650 and 1200 BC and compares it with the art of neighbouring lands may well be one of disappointment. This is the period which in Egypt produced the tomb-paintings of the earlier New Kingdom, the sensitive naturalism of the Amarna period, the opulence of the tomb of Tutankhamun, and the technical brilliance of the great battle-scenes of the Nineteenth Dynasty, while in the Aegean world the fresco-painting of the Minoan and Mycenaean palaces, the seal-stones of Crete, and the metalwork of the Shaft Graves have a notable place in any history of world art. In comparison to these Anatolia has only a little to offer. This may be partially due to the accidents of survival – there are no sumptuously appointed royal tombs, for instance, to provide 'treasures' which in other circumstances have perished. Yet it is also true that in such places as palaces and temples, buildings which in other areas were lavishly adorned with mural decoration, there is little indication that Hittite rulers felt any need for similar artistic effects. It has indeed been suggested that the decoration on Hittite relief vessels copied painted stucco reliefs on the walls of Hittite buildings, and that these in turn were inspired by Syro-Mesopotamian frescoes such as those at Mari and Alalah; but although some fragments of painted wall-plaster have been found at Hittite sites there is at present little evidence for pictorial wall-decoration. Only one building at Hattusas ('House 9' north-east of Temple VI in the southern part of the city) has yielded plaster fragments with a multi-coloured pattern which may include plant-motifs.[77] Small-scale works of art are comparatively few in number. It is not entirely surprising that the Hittites have been dubbed a people of 'sluggish emotions', 'intellectually unpretentious' and 'devoid of the finer graces'.[78]

125 Fragment of relief vase: man playing lute. From Boğazköy.

125

Relief sculpture

But if we do look in detail at those examples of Hittite art which have survived, it soon becomes clear that many of them possess qualities that should not be treated in such a dismissive way. There is in them a command of form and material, and a feeling of lively vigour, which

126–7 The Lion Gate,
Boğazköy.

gives them an attractive and immediately recognizable character of their own. This can best be seen in the low-relief rock-carvings which are to be found in many parts of Anatolia, and can be recognized as an original contribution to second millennium art. These survive in sufficient numbers to enable us to analyse the aims and techniques of Anatolian sculptors. They are for the most part carved on exposed faces of natural rock, which are cut back to form a smooth background from which the figures stand out in relief. In some cases the natural rock is replaced by cyclopean stonework in an architectural setting, as for instance on the sides of city gates; but in such situations the rock on which the carving is made is normally an essential part of the wall rather than a decorative slab externally applied to it. The result in both cases is that the sculpture becomes an integral part of its setting, and that the setting as a whole is an essential part of the work and gives it a power and vitality which can be overwhelming. Sometimes the artist has emphasized this unity of sculpture and setting by making the sculpture in a very real sense emerge from, rather than superimposing it on, the rock. Thus the gate-lions at Boğazköy have a convincing corporeality when seen in front view, but no attempt has been made to portray a side view visible as one passes through the gate. The same is true of the guardian sphinxes at Alaca, where the sides of the blocks have been used for entirely different figures. But perhaps the finest example of the technique is the 'sword-god' in Chamber B at Yazılıkaya. The symbolic meaning of this may not be entirely clear, but its effect on the viewer is immediate and powerful.

14, 15, 97,

126

127
128

119

128 The right-hand figure of the Sphinx Gate, Alaca. A double-headed eagle, on which a long-robed human figure is standing, can be seen on the side of the block.

129 Figure from the Sphinx
Gate, Boğazköy.

Some Hittite sculptures however show a different technique. The
129–30 gate-sphinxes from Boğazköy, unlike those at Alaca, are carved to
provide a side view as well as a frontal one, and the same is true of the
131–2 splendid figure of a lion seizing a calf, also from Alaca.

Sculptures are normally in low relief, but there are some exceptions.
32 The head of the figure on the King's Gate at Boğazköy, for instance,
shows almost three-quarters of the face standing out from the stone,
and the unused (and probably unfinished) figure abandoned on a
77 hillside at Fassılar protrudes so far as to be almost a sculpture in the

round. Within the low reliefs there are two very different techniques. Some sculptures are almost flat, with what little detail there is shown by engraved lines. In some cases they are so lacking in any kind of modelling that they have been suspected of being unfinished. In other sculptures (mainly in or near the capital) the relief is much more rounded and plastic, with a great deal of attention paid to the treatment of muscles, details of clothing and so on. Foreign influence, possibly Hurrian or Babylonian, has been suspected as the cause of this, but

133

130 Figure from the Sphinx Gate, Boğazköy.

there is little contemporary Mesopotamian relief with which to compare the Hittite examples, and it is equally possible that the technique was a development of a local school.

Hittite art is basically naturalistic, in the superficial sense that it portrays human beings, animals and occasionally objects. But this certainly does not mean that there is any attempt at portraiture, or at the portrayal of individual natural scenes. The art is rather 'idealistic' and 'conceptual' in the sense that the artist's aim is not to copy accurately what he sees before him but to convey with the maximum of

131 A lion holding a calf, from Alaca. This was probably a portal-figure, but its original position is uncertain. H. 99 cm.

132 Front view of the group shown above. Note the formalized decoration on the calf.

clarity what he considers to be the 'essence' of what he is carving. Thus in the conventional male figure the head is shown in profile whereas the shoulders and chest appear frontally; the legs and feet, however, are again in profile. These mixed figures are not the result of incompetence on the part of Hittite artists. They are in Hittite terms (and in the terms of other Middle Eastern art) ideal representations, showing what were regarded as the essential elements of 'manliness'. No attempt is made to show background or to relate the sculptures to a context other than that of the rock on which they are carved. The principal purpose is to evoke feeling rather than to portray fact.

Even when the carving of individual figures does not in itself have any great technical merit, the conventional position in which they are portrayed has several artistic advantages. First, it gives the impression of a steady, stately advance which adds life and movement to the sculptures. Second, and more important, it gives rise to the possibility of composition, either by the rhythmic repetition of figures to form a procession-like frieze or by the antithetical confrontation of two figures placed face to face. Both these techniques can be seen in the relief at Gavurkalesi, but by far the most elaborate example is in Chamber A at Yazılıkaya. Here the feeling of two columns advancing to meet at the focal point of the chamber is overwhelming. As a rule figures do not

15
114, 116

133 Rock-relief at Fraktin. On the left, Hattusilis III offers a libation to the Storm-god; on the right, Queen Puduhepa makes a similar offering to the goddess Hebat. H. of figures 1.30 m.

134 The restored Sphinx Gate at Alaca with casts of processional sculptures (ills. 136–41) in their original positions.

overlap and there is no attempt at three-dimensional representation, but in some groups the slow movement of the procession is speeded up to a controlled trot by overlapping the figures and slightly altering the position of their legs. The composition of the central group is more elaborate than this, for where the deities who lead the two processions meet face to face the dramatic unity of the scene is emphasized by the addition of opposed prancing bulls which can be seen *behind* the deities' legs on either side. Thus an unusual element of depth is given to the group at the expense, it has been pointed out, of theological accuracy, for in Hittite religion the bulls are the companions of the god and have no connection with the goddess.[79]

116

The finest example of Hittite pictorial composition, however, is in Chamber B. Again the starting-point is the conventional position, and the two figures, those of Tudhaliyas IV and his personal deity Sharruma, are in no way different from similar figures in Chamber A. But in the Chamber B relief the two are not merely juxtaposed. They are united in a way which is both emotionally powerful and artistically satisfying. In this case the figures are superposed with the god standing alongside the king, and the scale of the two is arranged so that the god, instead of holding the usual weapon in his left hand, clasps the right wrist of the king in a protective embrace. The organic coherence which this gives to the group is emphasized by the way in which the king's head fits into the curve of the god's shoulder. The whole forms a carefully organized composition, basically triangular but artistically

135, 117
120

modulated by the sweeping curves of the outline and the softly rounded modelling so that the god's extended right arm, the king's long garment and trailing *lituus*, the tilt of the high pointed hat and even the crescentic pommel of the sword are utilized and unified in a work of the very highest quality. It has to be emphasized that the idea of this grouping was not an inspiration on the part of the Yazılıkaya artist. A similar arrangement of king and protective deity had appeared on seals since the time of Muwatallis; but in the rock-carving at Yazılıkaya it achieved its final and finest expression.

The reliefs which have been discussed so far are concerned with religion, and are subject to hieratic conventions. Other sculptures deal with more secular subjects, and the rules which apply to them are in many ways different. This can be seen by an examination of the sculptures on either side of the Sphinx Gate at Alaca.[80] Some of these are typically 'processional', but others show acrobats, musicians and hunting scenes. The relationship between the two types is not completely clear, but it does seem likely that both would have been seen simultaneously on the same wall. The circus figures are a fairly clumsy attempt to escape from the rules applying to religious sculptures. In some instances (e.g. the sword-swallower or the man carrying a dog) the attempt almost succeeds, but in others it is a disastrous failure. The conventional pose makes it almost impossible to play a guitar or climb a ladder convincingly. But when the sculptor turns to animals the result is a work of much higher quality. In the hunting scenes a fine freedom of vigorous naturalistic movement is achieved by a bold use of outline, and this is attractively combined with a decorative formalism of such features as horns, manes and claws. Sometimes the decorative element is even extended to include the application of palmette motifs (e.g. on the haunches of the stags) and the provision of formalized 'vegetation' as scenery. In many ways the combination is more reminiscent of steppe-art than of that which we normally consider Hittite.

135 The figures of Tudhaliyas IV and Sharruma from Chamber B at Yazılıkaya (see ill. 119).

136–41 Sculptures from the Sphinx Gate at Alaca. *Below*: A king and queen worshipping a deity in the form of a bull, H. 1.27. *Over page, top left*: a group of acrobats; the figure on the right is climbing an unsupported ladder, while the one on the left is a sword-swallower, H. 1.17 m. *Below left*: a musician and a man carrying an animal (a dog or monkey?), H. 1.17 m. *Top right*: a hunting scene. *Centre right*: lion-hunting with dog, H. 1.29 m. *Bottom right*: stag-hunt, H. 80 cm.

Other art

A similar contrast between human and animal representation is to be seen in art products on a smaller scale. Vessels in the form of animals, notably the pair of bulls found on Büyükkale, have a lively and whimsical charm which is immediately attractive, and cult-rhyta both in clay and in precious metals achieve a high standard of vigorous naturalism. Statuettes of deities on the other hand tend to be much more formal and to follow in three dimensions the rules which apply to rock-relief. Of large-scale free-standing sculpture in stone very little survives. Perhaps if we had more than the feet of the huge statue mentioned in chapter 7 we would be able to praise the quality of Hittite sculpture in the round, but the almost completely rounded figure at Fassılar and the lower part of a statue found at Alaca do not inspire great confidence in the skills of local craftsmen. The features of the gate-figures at Boğazköy and the fragment of a more than life-size human head found at the same site suggest however that in the capital at least a much higher standard of workmanship was reached.

Outside Hittite territory there is little which can be included in a chapter on art. At Beycesultan, for instance, there is no sign that the inhabitants knew how to use a chisel, far less produce sculpture with it. Yet the impression given by this site may be misleading since further west at Sipylus and Karabel are rock-sculptures that look typically Hittite. These have often been taken to be memorials of conquest set up by Hittite kings, but the evidence available rather suggests that they were religious in purpose and carved on the orders of local monarchs. We may indeed be mistaken in thinking of Anatolian rock-sculpture as purely Hittite in style and origin. The little that we know of Old Kingdom sculpture suggests that it was in many ways different from that of the Imperial period, and it is possible that the development of the Imperial style was due to the introduction of elements from other areas, one of which may have been western Anatolia. Much more evidence is required before any final conclusions can be reached.

142 Bronze statuette of a god, from Tokat. The horns attached to the head rather than to the hat, and the position of the right arm, show that this figure does not conform completely to the Hittite tradition. H. 11.5 cm.

143 Head of a harnessed bull, from Tokat. H. 15.8 cm.

Literature

When we turn to the literary productions of the Hittite period it is necessary to clear our minds of possible misconceptions. Talk of 'literature' in an ancient Middle Eastern society does not imply the existence of works of creative imagination circulated to a reading public. A reading public simply did not exist. Nor can we accept that the literature we possess is what was preserved in written form at the end of a long tradition of popular oral literature. There is no evidence, for instance, that Hittite epic, though it does contain some 'formulaic' elements, is basically oral poetry 'frozen', as Homeric epic was, by the introduction of writing. On the contrary it seems clear that those elements are merely literary reminiscences of Mesopotamian technique, and that texts which we like to think of as literary were preserved only as part of the Mesopotamian system of training scribes in the art of writing. Much of this training took the form of copying texts, and in this connection there grew up a body of 'traditional' texts which were copied and re-copied in scribal schools all over the cuneiform world. 'Literary' texts formed a fairly small part of this collection, being far outnumbered by omen-texts, word-lists and similar documents. Why individual literary texts should have been included in the corpus is not clear, but it can be assumed that their survival is due much more to educational conservatism than to any desire to preserve works for their popularity or literary merit.

The same conservative attitude meant that there was a strong tendency towards word-for-word preservation of texts. However, the wording of many documents did vary with the passing of time, and in areas on the periphery of Mesopotamian civilization (as Hattusas was) adaptations were allowed to suit local scribal taste, translations of Mesopotamian texts into local languages were made, and at least some local material was added to the original corpus. The result is that literary texts preserved at Hattusas, although they are in many cases primarily Mesopotamian in conception, often have a 'flavour' which is recognizably Hittite. Thus the Gilgamesh epic appears in the Boğazköy archives not only in an Akkadian version, but also in translation into Hurrian and Hittite, and from what survives of the Hittite version it can be seen that those parts which dealt with the city of Uruk, and were presumably of interest mainly to a Mesopotamian audience, were shortened for Anatolian consumption, while the episode of the struggle with Huwawa, which was set in Hurrian territory far from the main centres of Mesopotamian learning, seems to have been expanded for the benefit of readers in that area, and suggests, like the translation into Hurrian, that the epic reached the Hittites through Hurrian intermediacy. Other foreign literary material is also predominantly Hurrian, although often there is evidence for Akkadian prototypes. In other instances the original is clearly Canaanite.[81]

144 Bronze statuette from Boğazköy. H. 12.7 cm.

The Kumarbi cycle

The best preserved texts concerned with a Hurrian milieu are those which deal with the god Kumarbi, his seizure of the kingship of the gods and his unsuccessful struggle to regain it after being replaced by

Teshub. The Kumarbi compositions are of interest not only for the parallels they provide for episodes in Hesiod and other Greek authors but also because they can be seen to have a metric structure. The normal line consists basically of two cola, in each of which there are two stressed and a varying number of unstressed syllables. This metric pattern is probably not a native growth, but is, like so much else, derived from Mesopotamia. Each line contains a single syntactical clause, and this with the habitual repetition of speeches and descriptions of incidents, gives the verse a measured dignity which can be seen only in a fairly long extract. This is given here in the translation of Professor H. G. Güterbock, who has followed the original as closely as possible, even at the expense of normal English word-order.

> *Kumarbi to Impaluri began to speak:*
> *'O Impaluri! The words which I speak to thee,*
> *To my words thine ear hold inclined!*
> *Into thy hand a staff take*
> *upon thy feet as shoes the swift winds put!*
> *And to the Irshirra-gods go,*
> *and these strong words before the Irshirras speak:*
> *"Come!*
>   *He calls you, Kumarbi, the gods' father, to the gods' house!*
> *But the matter about which he calls you*
> . . . .
> *Now come promptly."*
>
> *And the Irshirras will take him, the child,*
> *and they will carry him to the dark earth.*
> *But the Irshirras . . . .*
> *but not to the great gods will he be visible.'*
> *When Impaluri the words heard,*
> *into his hand the staff he took,*
> *upon his feet the shoes he put.*
> *And forth he travelled, Impaluri,*
> *and to the Irshirras he came.*
>
> *And Impaluri the words to the Irshirras again began to speak:*
> *'Come!*
>   *He calls you, Kumarbi, the gods' father!*
> *But the matter about which he calls you,*
> *that ye know not.*
> *Now hurry, come.'*
> *When the Irshirras the words heard,*
> *they hurried, hastened,*
> *and from their chair they rose.*
> *And at once they covered the way,*
> *and to Kumarbi they came.*
> *And Kumarbi to the Irshirras began to speak:*
> *'This child take,*
> *and as a gift treat him,*
> *and to the dark earth carry him!'*

And so the action moves gradually on. The pace is slow, but repetitions are seldom exact, and this helps to keep things moving and avoid monotony.

Native myths

Mythological texts of local origin do exist in the Hittite records, but it is clear that they are not works of literature in the same sense as those just discussed. Not only are they much less sophisticated both in detail and in over-all construction, but they are closely linked to cult and ritual in a way in which the foreign examples are not. The story of the Vanishing God and his return, for instance, is part of a ritual for regaining the good-will of a deity towards an individual, while the recital of the tale of the Storm-god's fight with the Dragon is part of the *purulli*-festival held at the holy city of Nerik. The texts are of the greatest interest to students of folk-lore and religion, but apart from an element of crude vigour their literary merit is extremely small.

Legend and history

As well as the epic-mythological past the Mesopotamian world was deeply interested in the semi-legendary past of the early historical monarchs. In this connection Sargon and Naram-Sin, the most powerful monarchs of the Dynasty of Akkad, were among the major figures, and an extensive literature grew up around them, some at least of which was translated into Hittite and included in the archives of Hattusas. But it is important to remember that the rulers of Akkad were remembered not merely for the greatness of their achievements but also for the disastrous ends to their reigns. In their lives Mesopotamian theologians saw a pattern of divine favour, human offence and divine retribution, which provided them with a systematic framework for the interpretation of history. This idea that the past was not a random succession of incidents but a pattern of connected events was something which the Hittites developed, again in their own characteristic way. For them, although divine favour was of supreme importance, disaster was due much less to its withdrawal than to human wickedness and mismanagement. So a native legend like that of the Siege of Urshu, which deals with the attempts of an early Hittite monarch to capture an enemy town, lays the blame for his lack of success neither on the gods nor on the king's failure to treat them correctly, but on the bungling incompetence of the generals involved and their inability to carry out their orders as instructed. In this instance there is no sign (at least in the surviving part of the story) that a moral was drawn for the benefit of contemporary generals, but from the earliest days of the Old Kingdom Hittite monarchs in their decrees can be seen explicitly making use of the past to point a moral for the present. Hattusilis I, for instance, in naming his grandson Mursilis I as his successor, orders his principal servants always to obey the royal words, for only in this way will Hattusas stand high and the land be at peace. In his grandfather's time that king's servants had disobeyed him and set a usurper on the throne. 'How many of them', asks the king rhetorically, 'escaped their fate?' Even more explicit is the opening of the Telepinus decree, where the king examines the early history of the realm and ascribes its success to the harmony which then existed in the royal family, while contemporary disasters are seen as resulting from the break-up of that harmony. In thus examining the past, stressing its value for the present and interpreting its patterns in terms of human behaviour rather than supernatural intervention, these early Hittite monarchs and their scribes have a reasonable claim to anticipate Herodotus in being described as Fathers of History.[82]

Other Herodotean features of Hittite court scribes are their talent for vivid narrative and their ability to create living characters. Their works consist mainly of decrees, annals and treaties, but even in these contexts they seldom strike the reader as being merely formal and conventional. On the contrary there is in them a gift for language which seems unforced and spontaneous, and a feeling for dramatic tension which can paint a scene or illustrate a character in an entirely original way. Typical examples are the craggy righteousness of Hattusilis I while his sister 'bellows like an ox' before him because her son is no longer heir to the throne; or the utter incredulity of Suppiluliumas when a messenger unexpectedly offers his son the throne of Egypt – 'Such a thing has never happened to me in my whole life!' Scenes such as these give official Hittite texts a life and a personal quality which is extremely attractive, and which certainly justifies their inclusion in a chapter on literature.

Prayers

Mention has been made in an earlier chapter (p. 116) of the prayers which are preserved in the Hittite archives. These texts too illustrate many of the points which have already been made. Their basic form and many of the concepts of them are, like so much else, borrowed from Mesopotamia, but in Hattusas they are adapted and infused with local feeling until they are transformed into something new. Although they do not show the originality of expression, the complexity of structure or the depth of religious thought which would give them any great literary stature, there is in them a genuine feeling of suffering and mental conflict, a simple straightforward philosophy of life, and a talent for homely unforced expression which makes them typically Hittite. Life, they say, is bound up with death and death with life. Man is mortal, and man is sinful. Even if a man is himself innocent the sins of his father fall upon him, he is afflicted by sickness and misery, and the anguish of his heart is impossible to endure. But when a man cries to a god for mercy the god listens to him, for god is merciful, a sheet-anchor in time of trouble. As a bird flies to its nest for refuge and the nest saves its life, so man seeks and finds refuge in god. 'Then beam on me like the full moon', cries the sufferer, 'shine over me like the sun in the sky; walk on my right hand; join with me like a yoked pair of oxen; walk by my side as a true god should.' One is reminded of King Tudhaliyas in the embrace of his protective deity in Chamber B at Yazılıkaya. But even in the midst of these figurative flights the Hittite worshipper retains his down-to-earth common sense. Divine self-interest alone, he points out to his deity, should be sufficient justification for his release from

120

suffering. After all, in killing off those who bring him offerings the god is in the end merely damaging himself. Much more to the point would be the transfer of the sufferings to enemy territory, where a supply of suitable scapegoats is conveniently available.

Songs

All the literature that has so far been mentioned belongs, as has been said, to the world of the royal court and the scribal schools. This is not to say that there was no unofficial popular literature. Doubtless songs were sung and tales were told not only in Hattusas but throughout Anatolia. A few lines of a soldiers' song are indeed preserved in a semi-historical text of the Old Kingdom period:

> *Nesas waspas, Nesas waspas*
> *tiya-mu, tiya.*
> *nu-mu annas-mas katta arnut;*
> *tiya-mu, tiya.*
> *nu-mu uwasmas katta arnut;*
> *tiya-mu, tiya.*
>
> *Clothes of Nesas, clothes of Nesas*
> *put on me, put!*
> *Bring down for me those of my mother;*
> *put on me, put!*
> *Bring down for me* (meaning uncertain);
> *put on me, put!*

The rhythmic structure and simple refrain strongly suggest a long tradition of popular poetry which may, if we accept the evidence of Hattian texts which seem to show some sort of stanza-division, go back to the pre-Hittite period. None of it, however, with the exception of this fragment, has been preserved. But when we remember that a ribald song sung by Julius Caesar's soldiers and preserved in Suetonius is practically the only evidence to be found in 'literary' Latin for a vast undercurrent of Roman popular song whose characteristic features did not come fully to the surface until the medieval period, it is easy to believe that a similarly large body of material existed in second-millennium Anatolia. But since it was of little interest to the staff of the temples and chancellery it was not normally recorded in writing and has now been irretrievably lost.

With literature we conclude our survey of the Anatolian Late Bronze Age during which the dominant position was held by the Hittites. Their rediscovery has revealed to us a people who, if they did not possess the genius and originality to change the course of world history, showed a talent for political and military organization, and a capacity to utilize their resources, which enabled them to gain, and retain for several hundred years, a leading position in the Middle Eastern world. Equally important, it has enabled us to see them not merely as remote people in a remote world but as real human beings with a personality and an individuality which we can still recognize after more than three thousand years.

9

Epilogue: Anatolia after the fall of the Hittite Empire

The break-up of the political units known to us as the Hittite Empire and Arzawa did not of course mean the complete elimination of all those who spoke the Indo-European languages of Anatolia. Linguistic and archaeological research-work is gradually dispelling the gloom of the Dark Age which followed the invasion of the 'Sea Peoples', and revealing the movements that took place within Anatolia, and the new political units which were formed. A great deal of work remains to be done, but it seems increasingly clear that we cannot now postulate four hundred years of chaos and an almost complete return to nomadic conditions. Anatolia continued to play an important part in the life of the Aegean and the Middle East. Its mineral and agricultural wealth were still an enormous attraction to neighbouring peoples, and the increasing use of iron after about 1200 BC served only to increase that attraction. The primary trade-routes of the preceding era can still be seen as the key to an understanding of the period, and while much has still to be learned about the states on and near the north-western route, the history of the struggle for the routes leading to the south-east can be reconstructed with a fair degree of certainty. The states involved in this struggle are for the most part new ones which rose to power in the political vacuum left by the collapse of the Hittite Empire, but in many cases their traditions and their language link them directly with their great predecessor.

1200–800: Neo-Hittites, Assyrians and Aramaeans

145 'Phrygian' pottery decoration. Alişar, eighth century BC.

The first indication of the new state of affairs is to be found in the records of Assyria. About 1160 BC the Assyrian provinces of Alzi and Puruhuzzi, situated (significantly?) in the area of the Erganı Maden copper-mines, were invaded by a great army of Muski from central Anatolia, and fifty years later an Assyrian counter-attack, led by Tiglath-Pileser I, had to deal not only with Muski but with Gasga as well. Clearly the Gasga had expanded from their northern homeland across central Anatolia since the fall of the Hittite Empire, and their allies the Muski probably came from the same direction. In the central area itself the archaeological evidence suggests a number of small principalities characterized by petty chieftains' castles and by the use of a new painted pottery usually known as 'Phrygian'. This pottery, [145] however, seems to have no connection with the west, and to be confined to central Anatolia until the eighth century. Theories derived from comparisons with Greek Geometric pottery which suggest that there was little or no occupation in central Anatolia until the same period do not seem to be borne out by the archaeological evidence, and may be based on false premises.

The Assyrian advance towards Anatolia was not confined to the Ergani Maden route. In 1110 Tiglath-Pileser I reached the Malatya region and encountered a kingdom called Milid which he refers to as Hatti. On another campaign he had contact with another king of Hatti, probably at Carchemish, and it can be seen that these and other political units claiming to be the successors of the Hittite Empire had by this time reorganized themselves round the old trade-routes and river-crossings. Inscriptions from these states show that their language was a Luwian dialect written in 'Anatolian Hieroglyphs', and it may be assumed that their population was a combination of local peoples and Luwian-speaking groups driven from the plateau by the advance of the Gasga and the Muski. Both of these elements had been part of the Hittite Empire long enough to consider themselves its natural heirs.

Strategically placed as they were, the 'Neo-Hittite' states could not expect their control of the trade-routes to go unchallenged. Assyrian encroachments about 1100 have already been mentioned, and soon after this a new danger appeared in the shape of the Aramaeans, nomads from east of the Euphrates who succeeded in seizing several Hittite principalities and establishing themselves in them. The Aramaean incursions had a serious effect on the Assyrians as well as the Hittite states, and it was not until after 900 BC that Assyrian armies again reached northern Syria and began to penetrate the mountains of Anatolia. For a century the north Syrian states were subjected to a constant series of Assyrian campaigns which produced large amounts of tribute but no permanent conquest. On the Anatolian plateau the Muski were still active in the areas overlooking the Syrian plain, but in the background we can begin to see what must have been the principal power of central Anatolia – the land of Tabal. This state, Luwian-speaking and centred probably on the region of modern Kayseri, was to play an increasing part in the struggle for the trade-routes. Its relation to the producers of the painted 'Phrygian' pottery mentioned above is still problematical, but to call this pottery 'Tabalian' is perhaps less likely to be wrong than to use the name 'Phrygian' for it.

The first Assyrian monarch to come into contact with Tabal was Shalmaneser III, who after reducing the more southerly Neo-Hittite states crossed the Amanus in 839 BC and advanced through what had once been called Kizzuwadna and was now known as Que. The cities of Kizzuwadna and Lawazantiya (near modern Şar and Elbistan) fell to him, and two years later he was able to cross the Anti-Taurus, destroy the cities of Tabal, and receive the submission of its kings. The most important of these rulers was called Tuwatis, a monarch whose inscription in hieroglyphs has survived at Topada. After his victory Shalmaneser turned south-west towards Hubusni (modern Ereğli) and returned through the Cilician Gates and across the Amanus again.

800–700: Urartu and Muski

One of the less expected results of centuries of Assyrian and Aramaean pressure on the hills to their north was the enforced union of a number of hitherto independent peoples of the Armenian mountains and beyond into a state known as Urartu. By about 800 this new power was becoming sufficiently strong to extend its influence westwards towards Milid, Tabal and other Luwian-speaking states. This eventually brought Urartu face to face with Assyria, and when in 743 the vital battle was fought the Assyrians emerged as victors. From then on Urartu was no longer a serious rival in the struggle for the resources of Anatolia, and without her support the Neo-Hittite states of northern Syria were unable to resist Assyrian pressure and were quickly absorbed.

This brought Assyrian forces once more to the borders of Anatolia, where Tabal, now ruled by Washu-Sharma, was still the dominant state. Allied to Tabal were several smaller kingdoms clustered round the routes through the Taurus – Tuhana (near modern Niğde) whose ruler Warpalawas has left us his portrait and hieroglyphic inscription at Ivriz, Atuna (near Bulgar Maden), Ishtunda (possibly Karatepe on the River Ceyhan), and Hupisna (perhaps at modern Ereğli). Gasga too were still present, though their precise location is unknown. South of the Taurus and Anti-Taurus mountains lay Que under its king Urikki, in an area more open to Assyrian attack. At first these states were quick to submit, but this was only temporary, for about 730 Washu–Sharma of Tabal failed to pay his tribute, and so was deposed and was replaced by the pro-Assyrian Hulli, 'son of nobody'.

Even this was not sufficient to ensure the loyalty of the Anatolian kingdoms. By 718 there was further trouble in Tabal, and a new anti-Assyrian coalition had been formed consisting of Tabal itself, the Muski under their ruler Mita, and even the king of Carchemish. Assyrian reaction was inevitable. Carchemish was captured while Mita was still trying to fight his way through Que, then Mita was driven back and defeated in his own province, and finally Hulli of Tabal was replaced by his son Ambaris, who was diplomatically married to an Assyrian princess and given the province of Hilakku, probably round modern Karaman, as a dowry. Finally in 713 Ambaris too was deposed and Tabal became an Assyrian province.

700–600: Cimmerians, Phrygians and Lydians

The fall of the most important kingdom of central Anatolia meant that Mita of Muski, defeated but unconquered, was the only survivor of the original alliance. Surprisingly enough, when he next emerges, it is as a friend of the Assyrian king, for when in 709 Urikki, the presumably exiled ex-king of Que, despatched emissaries to make contact with Urartu in an attempt to stir up trouble for the Assyrians, they were intercepted on their way through Mita's territory and generously handed over to the Assyrians. The motives which lay behind Mita's sudden change of heart are obscure, but it may well have been prompted by events beyond his control further to the north and east. In

714 the Cimmerians, a horde of fierce warriors from southern Russia, broke through the Caucasus and descended on Urartu. From there they turned west along the south shore of the Black Sea, set up a base in the vicinity of Sinope, and moved southwards towards Tabal. Any reconstruction of the events of the next few years is full of uncertainties, but the effect of this movement must have been to compress Mita between two hostile forces. Hence his sudden desire for friendship with Assyria. His gesture of reconciliation was apparently accepted, for it seems clear that the Assyrians then felt that they could rely on him for help in subduing the few remaining neo-Hittite principalities. But even an alliance of Mita with the Assyrians was unable to check the Cimmerian pressure. In 705 an Assyrian army, possibly including the forces of Mita, was heavily defeated somewhere in central Anatolia, the Assyrian king was killed in action, and Mita of Muski disappears from our records. What happened to him is unknown, but it is at least possible that he and his forces escaped from the disaster and fled from central Anatolia along the old route to the west. Thus Mita of Muski may have vanished from the Assyrian border-lands and emerged on the periphery of the Greek world as Midas of Phrygia.

It need hardly be said that this account of the history of King Midas is the author's personal interpretation of the evidence, and differs widely from that usually suggested. The 'standard' reconstruction, based on the accounts preserved by Greek folk-memory, assumes that the Bryges or Phrygians crossed into Anatolia from south-eastern Europe shortly before the Trojan War. The presence of Muski about 1150 on the upper Tigris and Euphrates can then be seen as evidence of the furthest penetration of this European people. However no archaeological evidence has been found to support such far-reaching activity, and in fact when evidence becomes more abundant it points much more strongly to a movement from east to west, rather than in the other direction. Certainly there are signs of movements into Anatolia from south-east Europe around 1200 BC. In the north-west the site of Troy (level VIIb2) shows the introduction of crude hand-made pottery known as Knobbed Ware which seems to have an ultimate affinity with

146 'Knobbed Ware'. Troy VIIb.

𐤔𐤉𐤌𐤀𐤏𐤎𐤀𐤊𐤏𐤉

147 Inscription incised in
wax which was smeared on
to a bronze bowl. Gordion,
eighth century BC.

wares of the Late Bronze Age in Hungary and central Europe. Further
east, at the later Phyrgian capital of Gordion in the Sangarius valley,
hand-made black pottery appears at about the same time. The two
wares are not directly related, but may have a similar ultimate origin. At
Gordion the new pottery is introduced without any signs of a break in
the continuity of the site, and quickly disappears as though the
newcomers to the site had been absorbed. In fact Gordion seems, from
the limited evidence at present available, to have developed peacefully
and virtually without interruption, and it is difficult to see in the makers
of the black hand-made pottery a conquering aristocracy who swept
across Anatolia to the frontiers of Assyria.

Despite the continuity at Gordion, there are signs of large-scale
movements in western Anatolia between 1200 and 700 BC. Troy VIIb2
was destroyed about 1100 BC, and in the south-west the site of
Beycesultan (level I) was destroyed about 1000 BC and not reoccupied.
Historical records when they become available again show a pattern of
occupation completely different from what it had been in the Late
Bronze Age, but there is a curious similarity of names which must have
some historical explanation. Lycians, Carians and Mysians may well be
the descendants of the inhabitants of Bronze Age Lukka, Karkisa and
Masa, but it must not be too readily assumed that the areas which they
occupied in the Classical period were identical with those in which they
lived in the Hittite era. It may well be that in the dark period after 1200
they were forced from their former homes and pushed west and south
into the areas in which they were later to be found. The pressure behind
this movement presumably came from Europe, but no details of those
who exerted it are known. It was perhaps at this time that groups such
as the Mygdones, the tribe of the Phrygian eponymous hero Mygdon,
crossed into Anatolia and settled in the region of modern Iznik and the
lower Sangarius valley, driving the original inhabitants (the Masa)
from their homes and starting a movement which ended only when
Lukka-people reached Lycia in the far south-west. In their new homes
these peoples continued to use their Luwian dialects, as can be seen
from inscriptions written by them in the Classical period. In these
'Late Luwian' kingdoms we can in fact see that last survivors in western
Anatolia of the political units of the second millennium.

Where Phrygia is concerned, its capital city Gordion remains a
typically western Anatolian town until the late eighth century, when
there is a rapid increase of eastern influence in the shape of painted
pottery, cauldrons of Urartian type, and fibulae which have
connections with south-east Anatolia and northern Syria. Most
important of all is perhaps the appearance of alphabetic writing in
conjunction with these eastern features at a period which antedates any
Greek import to Gordion.[83] This writing-system must have had its
origins to the south-east, and although independent borrowing of a
Semitic script by Phrygians and Greeks remains a likely hypothesis,[84] it
is at least possible that the development of the alphabet from the
Phoenician system of writing, and its introduction to Greece, did not
take place only through Greek contacts in Levantine ports, as has long
been supposed. It may be that the original inspiration towards

148

147

alphabetic writing took place in south-east Anatolia, where Phoenician and Luwian were written and spoken side by side (as for instance in the Karatepe bilingual), and that when Assyrian and Cimmerian pressure forced monarchs such as Mita of Muski towards the north-west they brought with them not only bowls and safety-pins but the new script as well. From Gordion it could have been passed on to the Greek settlements on the Aegean coast (Midas is said to have married a princess of Cyme in Aeolis), and from there to the western world.

148 Phrygian fibula from Gordion, eighth century BC.

The scanty evidence of the Phrygian language which has survived suggests that Phrygian, like the tongues of the other Anatolian states of the time, is basically a member of the Hittite-Luwian group. In following the further history of this group we find that the dominance of Midas of Phrygia did not last long, for shortly after 700 the Cimmerians followed him to his new capital and forced him to commit suicide. At the same time they advanced southwards through Tabal until in 679 they were stopped by the Assyrians just north of the Cilician Gates. For the next fifty years they kept up a constant pressure, with the result that the kingdoms of Tabal and Hilakku were forced into a policy of alternate resistance to Assyria and appeals to her for help. Further west the fall of Gordion had left the leadership of western Anatolia vacant, and the position was now filled by Lydia, a state situated in what had once been the centre of Arzawa. Linguistically Lydian too is related to the Hittite-Luwian group, but the curious thing is that unlike most of its contemporaries it seems to be a descendant of the Hittite rather than of the Luwian sub-branch. One has to assume that in the disturbances following the collapse of the Hittite Empire a central Anatolian group had seized power among the ruins of Arzawa, and a memory of this may be preserved in the Herodotean story of a Heraclid dynasty with eastern connections which gained power in Lydia about 1200 BC. One king of this dynasty has the name of Myrsilus, and we may see in him a late descendant and namesake of the Hittite king Mursilis.

By about 660 BC Lydia too was forced to seek Assyrian help against the Cimmerians, and although a temporary respite was gained, it was not until about 630 that the Assyrians were able to defeat the invaders in the south-east, while Lydia was not freed from them until about 610.

Finale: Medes, Persians and after

With the final defeat of the Cimmerians the native kingdoms of central Anatolia regained their independence, for by this time Assyrian power had been finally broken by events nearer home. The principal beneficiary was Hilakku, while the Lydians were able to advance as far as the Halys in an attempt to fill the gap left by the Assyrian departure. But Anatolia was too important to be left alone for long. In 612 Assyria fell to the Medes and Babylonians, and by 600 the Babylonians were in Cilicia (known to them as Hume), while the Medes were advancing through the Armenian mountains. By 585 the Medes had penetrated as far as the Halys, where they met and fought a drawn battle with the Lydians. At the peace-talks that followed the arbitrators were, according to Herodotus, 'Labynetus of Babylon' and 'Syennesis of Cilicia' – presumably the Babylonian governor of Hume and the king of Hilakku. Again peaceful conditions returned for a few years until in 550 Cyrus of Persia defeated and deposed the king of Media and so created another vacuum in central Anatolia. Croesus of Lydia was quick to cross the Halys in an attempt to gain what he could, and at the same time Cyrus led his army through the mountains to defend the empire he had seized. On this occasion the arbitrators in the 585 agreement took opposite sides, Hilakku favouring Cyrus while Babylon supported Croesus. In 546 Croesus was defeated and the Lydian kingdom was incorporated into the Persian Empire. Hilakku's support of Cyrus was rewarded by the gift of Hume, and it was now for the first time that the name Hilakku/Cilicia was applied to the coastal plain south of the Taurus Mountains. For almost a hundred and fifty years Cilicia was a vassal-kingdom within the Persian Empire until it was fully incorporated and became a province in 401.

The Persian conquest of Anatolia really brings the political history of its Hittite-Luwian-speaking peoples to an end. In central Anatolia the Greeks knew of groups whom they called 'White Syrians', and it may be that this name was given to them because they spoke the same language as the Greeks had found when they first reached Syria – the hieroglyphic Luwian of the Neo-Hittite kingdoms. In western and southern Asia Minor from Caria to Cilicia it can be seen that Hittite-Luwian languages were spoken throughout the Classical period, and traces of them have been found surviving into the Christian era. In the survival of the native language of Isauria, as recorded by patristic writers of the sixth century AD, we can perhaps see the final remnant of a linguistic movement into Anatolia which had taken place more than three thousand years before.

Notes on the text

For abbreviations see Bibliography, p. 167.

1   The type site is still Arpachiyah, near Mosul. See M. E. L. Mallowan and J. Cruikshank Rose, *Prehistoric Assyria; the Excavations at Tell Arpachiyah* (1935). For a comparison with Anatolia cf. J. Mellaart, *Earliest Civilizations of the Near East* (1965), 125, modified by him in *CAH³* I, l, 281.

2   The impression that the northern half of the Anatolian plateau was undeveloped, indeed virtually uninhabited, in the Neolithic period may in the end prove to be false. There is, for instance, evidence of Neolithic occupation near the site of Demirci Hüyük, in the Eskişehir plain. Here Neolithic sherds were found in the mud of house-walls built in the third millennium BC. They must have been dug up somewhere near the site when this mud was excavated for construction purposes. Since virgin soil at the site is some 7.5 m below the present ground surface, it seems that here, and possibly in many other areas, erosion of soil from the surrounding hills and its deposit in the plains and river valleys may have caused the covering of early sites to a depth which makes it virtually impossible to recognize them from surface indications.

3   See for instance the development at Eridu; S. Lloyd and F. Safar, *Sumer* IV (1948), 115 ff.; S. Lloyd, *ILN*, 31 May 1947, 581 ff.; *ILN*, 11 September 1948, 303 ff.

4   A treasure of Troy II type has also been reported from Dorak, not far from Bursa in north-west Anatolia. It was illustrated by drawings in *ILN*, 28 November 1959, but has since disappeared. No photographs are available, and doubts have been cast on its authenticity. It is therefore prudent not to rely on its evidence unless it reappears and is recognized as genuine.

5   Proposals have from time to time been made for the lowering of the date usually accepted for the Trojan 'treasures' (and for the destruction of Level IIg, in which they were almost certainly found) on the basis of comparisons with Mesopotamia and Crete. See for instance S. Hood, *Bericht über den V internationalen Kongress für Vor- und Frühgeschichte, Hamburg, 1958* (1961), 398–403; R. Maxwell-Hyslop, *Western Asiatic Jewellery c. 3000–612 BC* (1971), 57–60; P. Calmeyer, 'Das Grab eines Altassyrischen Kaufmanns', *Iraq* XXXIX (1977), 87–97. But comparative dating by the use of metalwork is of doubtful value. Metal objects, especially precious objects, can travel over long distances as gifts or booty, and can be preserved for centuries as family heirlooms. It is dangerous to assume that the manufacture of any such object can be assigned either to the area in which it happens to be found or to the date of the context in which it is found.

6   H. Frankfort, *The Art and Architecture of the Ancient Orient* (1970), 211 ff.

7   C. L. Woolley, *Ur Excavations*, Vol. II, *The Royal Cemetery* (1934). See also P. R. S. Moorey's up-to-date revision of Woolley's popular account, *Ur 'of the Chaldees'* (1982), 51–103.

8   M. E. L. Mallowan, 'Excavations at Brak and Chagar Bazar', *Iraq* 9 (1947), 1 ff.

9   B. Landsberger, *JNES* 24 (1965), 285–96. For a persuasive suggestion that the metal in question was neither tin nor lead, but a high-arsenic-content copper, see H. McKerrell, *The Use of Tin-bronze in Britain and the Comparative Relationship with the Near East* in A. D. Franklin, J. S. Olin and T. H. Wertime (eds), *The Search for Ancient Tin* (1978), 7–24.

10   This theory has been proposed, and extensively developed, by Marija Gimbutas. See for instance her chapter in G. Cardona, H.

M. Hoenigswald and A. Senn (eds), *Indo-European and Indo-Europeans* (1970), 155–97. Other areas for a 'homeland' have been proposed – the Hungarian plain, for instance, and North Germany/Scandinavia. These areas however are much less probable, and there is little or no archaeological evidence to support them.

11   Other routes are of course possible, though much less likely. It was for instance suggested by C. L. Woolley (in *A Forgotten Kingdom*, 1953, 29–35) on the basis of the presence of 'Khirbet Kerak' pottery in widely separated areas, that the ancestors of the Hittites moved from the south Caucasus area *via* north Mesopotamia to the Amuq plain near the borders of Syria and Turkey. Thence some crossed the Amanus and Anti-Taurus ranges to the Hittite 'homeland' in central Anatolia, while others migrated southwards to become the Palestinian Hittites of the Old Testament.

12   See for instance L. R. Palmer, *Mycenaeans and Minoans* (1965), 246 ff.

13   J. Mellaart, *CAH*³ I, 2, 406 ff.; M. J. Mellink in R. W. Ehrich (ed.), *Chronologies in Old World Archaeology* (1965), 115 ff.; J. G. Macqueen, *Acta of the 2nd. International Colloquium on Aegean Prehistory* (1972), 142–5. Mellaart also was earlier (*AJA* 62, 1958, 9–33) in favour of an overlap.

14   M. Gimbutas in G. Cardona, H. N. Hoenigswald and A. Senn (eds), *Indo-European and Indo-Europeans* (1970), 164–8.

15   C. J. Gadd in *CAH*³ I, 2, 426 ff.

16   J. Mellaart, *AJA* 62 (1958), 14.

17   Compare for instance the *megaron*-buildings of Troy I and II (C. W. Blegen, *Troy and the Trojans*, 1963, 44 and 65), and the *megaron* in Beycesultan XXIV (S. Lloyd and J. Mellaart, *Beycesultan* I, 1962, 24–6).

18   The arrival of this pottery in central Anatolia has also been equated with that of Hittite-speakers. See J. Mellaart, *CAH*³ I, 2, 694; R. A. Crossland, ibid. 845.

19   W. F. Albright and T. O. Lambdin, *CAH*³ I, 1, 142. The suggestion has little to recommend it.

20   J. Mellaart, *AJA* 62 (1958), 20–21.

21   R. J. Howell in R. A. Crossland and A. Birchell (eds), *Bronze Age Migrations in the Aegean* (1973), 73 ff.

22   D. H. French, *AnSt* XVII (1967), 62–3. French consequently re-names the Anatolian ware 'Inegöl Grey Ware'.

23   J. B. Haley and C. W. Blegen, *AJA* 32 (1928), 141 ff.

24   These references are complicated by the use in Hittite texts of the word *Labarnas* as a royal title. Hittite scribes of the Imperial period, in reconstructing their own earlier history, saw *Labarnas* as in origin the name of an early king, a predecessor of Hattusilis I. Many reconstructions of Hittite history therefore place a 'Labarnas' at the head of the line of Hittite kings. But there is very little evidence for his independent existence, and it can be reasonably assumed, as here, that events attributed to his reign in fact took place during the reign of Hattusilis.

25   See M. B. Rowton, *CAH*³ I, 1, 212 ff.; N. Na'aman *AnSt* XXVI (1976), 128–43. The literature on the subject is extensive.

26   E. Laroche, *RA* 1976, 18.

27   M. J. Mellink, *AJA* 87 (1983), 138–41.

28   V. Hankey, *Asian Affairs* V (1974), 54.

29   For instance by D. L. Page, *History and the Homeric Iliad* (1959), many of whose conclusions have been invalidated by the more recent re-dating of crucial texts. The position has recently been strongly re-stated by H. G. Güterbock in *AJA* 87 (1983), 133–8.

30   Two points are worth mentioning here: (i) There is in the extensive documentation from Ugarit no sign of any name which is recognizably Mycenaean Greek. This has led to the suggestion that Mycenaean goods, which were plentiful in Ugarit as elsewhere along the Syrian and Palestinian coasts, were not brought directly to the area in Mycenaean ships, but were off-loaded at Cypriot ports, and re-loaded on to Cypriot or Syrian vessels for shipment further east. If this was the case, the argument for the ships of Ahhiyawa, which are known to have traded with and through north Syria, being equated with Mycenaen vessels, loses much of its validity. (ii) An indication of what *the Egyptians* called the Mycenaean Greeks may be gained from an inscription on a statue-base in the funerary temple of Amenophis III in Western Thebes. On the left of a cartouche of Pharaoh there is a list of twelve names: (1) *imnš*; (2) *byš*[*t?*]; (3) *ktny*; (4) *mkn*; (5) *dḳis*; (6) *mḍni*; (7) *npry*; (8) *ktr*; (9) *wiry*; (10) *knš*; (11) *imnš*; (12) *rkt*. Of these names, it can be plausibly suggested that five, possibly six, are recognizable as being places in Crete: Amnisos (1 *and* 11 [!]), Phaestos (2), Kydonia (3), Knossos (10), Lyktos (12), and Dikte [???] (5). One other is the island of Cythera (8), and three – Mycenae (4), Messenia (6) and Nauplia (7) – are in Mycenaean Greece. To the right of the cartouche are two further names: *kftiw* and *tny*.

There is almost universal agreement that the first of these refers to Crete, which presumably means that the second is a general name for the remaining places – i.e. that *tny* = Mycenaean Greece. This has led many to equate *tny* with the land of the Danaoi, one of the names for the Greeks in the Homeric poems. This equation is by no means certain. But whether it is correct or not, the text does seem to show that as far as the Egyptians were concerned (at least around 1370, the date of the death of Amenophis III), the Mycenaean Greeks were not called Achaeans, or anything remotely resembling Achaeans. If we turn now to the attacks of the 'Sea Peoples' some 150–200 years later, we find among the invaders *c.* 1186 the *dnyn*, who may well be the same people as the *tny* of the earlier text. If this is the case, and if the *dnyn/tny* are to be recognized as the Mycenaean Greeks, as the statue-base text suggests, then it seems unlikely that the *ikws*, who were allies of the Libyans in an earlier attack by 'Sea Peoples' on Egypt *c.* 1218, were also Mycenaean Greeks. It seems more probable that if they can be identified at all they are to be taken as coming from Anatolian Ahhiyawa, and that they, and their name, have no connection with the Mycenaeans.

Observant readers will have noticed that this discussion has omitted one of the names on the statue-base of Amenophis III – no. 9: *wiry*. This has been interpreted as an Egyptian version of (W)ilion/Troy. Presumably for the Egyptians *wiry* was part of either *kftiw* or *tny*. If the identification with Troy is correct, then Troy must have been considered by the Egyptians to be part of either the Cretan or the Mycenaean world. For a Cretan connection for Troy there is no evidence at all, and so one would have to assume that Troy was a town of *tny*, of the Mycenaeans. But though there are clear signs of Mycenaean contacts with Troy, these indicate only a trading relationship, and there is nothing to suggest that late Troy VI, which was contemporary with Amenophis, was either a Mycenaean settlement or under the political control of Mycenaeans from mainland Greece. I therefore doubt if *tny* can with any degree of probability be extended to north-west Anatolia, and am more inclined to think that *wiry* is, in fact, a still unidentified settlement either on Crete or on the mainland of Mycenaean Greece.

For recent discussion of the statue-base, with relevant bibliographical information, see J. Strange, *Caphtor/keftiu; a New Investigation* (1980), 21 ff; J. D. Muhly in J. D. Muhly, R.

Maddin, V. Karageorghis (eds), *Early Metallurgy in Cyprus, 4000–500* BC (1982), 260 f.

31 For many years one of the difficulties in disagreeing with the identification of Ahhiyawa with Mycenaean Greece has been that no reasonable alternative identification could be proposed. If the influence of Ahhiyawa was strongly felt in western Anatolia, and even reached the Syrian coast, and Ahhiyawa was *not* Mycenaean Greece, then what *was* it? Some fragments of north-west Anatolian pottery have been found in the Levant; but they scarcely add up to a major power such as Ahhiyawa must have been. Although one can get round this by arguing that Ahhiyawan trade was in perishable goods, there almost certainly is not room in north-western Turkey for a 'great power' of the Late Bronze Age. But in recent years, work in Turkey-in-Europe and the south-east Balkans has shown that on the European side of the straits there is indeed evidence for a power capable of standing on an equal footing with the better-known monarchies of the Late Bronze Age world. See for instance R. F. Hoddinott, *The Thracians* (1981), especially chapter 3. Nothing so far, it must be admitted, suggests any extensive trading-connections between Thrace and the Levant; but future work may change this picture. We are still in the realms of guesswork. But Ahhiyawa may in the end be seen to have lain in Thrace, or mainly in Thrace, rather than in Greece or in the Aegean world.

32 J. Mellaart, *AnSt* XVIII (1968), 187 ff.

33 J. D. Muhly, *AJA* 89 (1985), 281, with references.

34 Contact is shown by the presence of 'ingot-torcs', riveted daggers and other features in both regions. See S. Piggot, *Ancient Europe* (1965), 102 and Fig. 56.

35 See note 32.

36 It may be possible to reach conclusions on local tin-sources from the tin-content of ancient slags. See for instance P. S. de Jesus, *The Development of Prehistoric Mining and Metallurgy in Anatolia* (1980), 55–6.

37 The re-dating of these texts was at first based on internal evidence, e.g. the presence of a 'king of the Hurrians' at a time when the Hurrian kingdom had ceased to exist (*CAH*[3] II, 1, 676–7). More recently it has become increasingly possible to distinguish texts of different periods because of differences both in 'spelling' and in the forms of cuneiform characters.

38 An alternative possibility is that Arzawa ceased to exist as a separate political entity, and that its territory was divided among the other 'Arzawa lands'. See S. Heinhold-Krahmer, *Arzawa* (1977), 136 ff.; I. Singer, *AnSt* XXXIII (1983), 206.

39 This reconstruction is based on the assumption that the 'Tawagalawas Letter' (*KUB* XIV, 3) is to be dated to the latter part of the reign of Mursilis. See J. G. Macqueen, *AnSt* XVIII (1968), 180. Others assign the text to Muwatallis (O. R. Gurney, *The Hittites*³ (1980), 52, or to Hattusilis III (I. Singer, *AnSt* XXXIII, 1983, 209–10), and events have to be reconstructed accordingly.

40 J. Garstang and O. R. Gurney, *The Geography of the Hittite Empire* (1959), 73. For an alternative location see K. Bittel, *Hattusha, Capital of the Hittites* (1970), 21. A carved figure and inscription of Muwatallis at Meydancik Kalesi in Cilicia Tracheia (E. Laroche, *AJA* 78, 1974, 111) may well indicate that this site was within the boundaries of the Land of Tarhun-tassa; but it is unlikely that it was the town of Tarhuntassa itself to which Muwatallis moved.

41 For accounts of the battle see, for instance, Y. Yadin, *The Art of Warfare in Biblical Lands* (1963), 103 ff.; C. W. Ceram, *Narrow Pass, Black Mountain* (1956), 160 ff. The battle took place in the fifth year of Rameses II. This I have taken to be 1286, but Egyptian chronology is still sufficiently uncertain to make several other dates (1300, 1275, 1272) possible.

42 The opposite view is maintained by I. Singer (*AnSt* XXXIII, 1983, 214), who sees the absence of reference to western states as indicating 'relatively peaceful circumstances, or perhaps even a more centralised incorporation within the Hittite lands'. It is difficult to believe that this would result in the entire disappearance of western names from the records.

43 For recent treatments of the subject of the Sea Peoples see V. Hankey, *Asian Affairs* NS V (1974), 51 ff.; J. Mellaart, *Mansel'e Armağan (Mélanges Mansel)* (1974), 493 ff.; N. K. Sandars, *The Sea Peoples* (1985). Caution should be exercised in making facile identifications of Sea Peoples with the inhabitants, or prospective inhabitants, of such distant areas as Sicily, Sardinia and Etruria.

44 A. Goetze, *CAH*³ II, 2, 266.

45 The idea of a Hittite monopoly of iron comes from an unwarranted interpretation of a Hittite document (*KBo* I, 14) which mentions a request for iron made by a foreign monarch. For details of the text see A. Goetze, *Kizzuwatna and the Problem of Hittite Geography* (1940), 27–33.

46 The identification of the site of Inandık, some 25 miles south of Çankırı, as Hanhana (K. Balkan, *Belleten* 164, 1977, 649–52) is not entirely convincing. It is based on the mention of a governor of Hanhana on a tablet found there. But there is nothing in other texts to indicate that Hanhana was west of the Halys, and its close association with sites such as Nerik makes it difficult, if not impossible, to locate it there. An additional problem is that Inandık is Old Hittite in date, while Hanhana was prominent in the Empire period.

47 Situation at Havza, J. G. Macqueen, *AnSt* XXX (1980), 179–87; at Oymaağaç, *AnSt* XXIII (1973), 64; J. Yakar, *MDOG* 112 (1980), 84. The suggestion of a situation near the sharp bend of the Halys opposite Kargı (H. G. Güterbock, *JNES* 20, 1961, 93) is attractive, but the area (like that of Havza) has as yet yielded no remains of the appropriate period.

48 Location on Halys, J. Garstang and O. R. Gurney, *The Geography of the Hittite Empire* (1959), 36; on Euphrates, S. Alp, *Anatolia* I (1956), 77 ff.

49 Y. Yadin, *The Art of Warfare in Biblical Lands* (1963), 3.

50 K. Bittel, *RA* 1976, 9–14. One is tempted to ask: have we here a portrait of an Ahhiyawan warrior?

51 C. W. Blegen, *Troy* III, 1 (1953), 96.

52 See for instance P. Stirling, *Turkish Village* (1965); J. E. Pierce, *Life in a Turkish Village* (1964).

53 L. R. Palmer, *Achaeans and Indo-Europeans* (1955), 14; O. R. Gurney, *CAH*³ II, 1, 253 ff. For another view see S. Piggott, *Ancient Europe* (1965), 81.

54 J. G. Macqueen, *AnSt* IX (1959), 181; O. R. Gurney, *CAH*³ II, 1, 667 ff.

55 S. R. Bin-Nun, *The Tawananna in the Hittite Kingdom* (1975), 102.

56 Because of the restricted nature of such sites, it has been suggested that these buildings were not permanent residences, but rather fortified places of refuge for use in times of danger. See R. Naumann in *Beiträge zur Altertumskunde Kleinasiens* (1983), 390.

57 (a) H. Goldman, *AJA* 41 (1937), 284. (b) H. Goldman, *Excavations at Gözlü Kule, Tarsus* II (1956), 29.

58 C. W. Blegen, *Troy and the Trojans* (1963), 154. The way in which I have expanded

Blegen's comment is of course only a light-hearted parody of the way in which efforts have over the years been made to link the archaeology and topography of the area of 'Troy' (we might really be better to refer to the site as Hissarlık in order to avoid begging the question) to the information provided in the Homeric poems. Thus the storage jars buried in the floors of Level VIIa (see page 71) are taken to be indications that the settlement was under siege at the time. In the last few years many long-held theories, particularly the one which has placed the Greek camp to the north of the site on the shores of the Hellespont and the principal battles in the area between there and the north side of 'Troy', have had to be abandoned since it has become clear (G. R. Rapp, ed., *Troy; the Archaeological Geology*, 1982) that almost all that area was under the shallow water of a lagoon at the time of the 'Trojan War'.

59 K. Bittel, *Hattusha, Capital of the Hittites* (1970), 85.
60 C. Mora, *SMEA* 18 (1977), 227–37.
61 P. S. de Jesus, *Archäologie und Naturwissenschaften* 2 (1981), 95–105.
62 D. L. Giles and E. Kuijpers, *Science* 186 (29 Nov. 1974), 823–5.
63 G. F. Bass, *TAPS* 57, 8 (1967); G. F. Bass, D. A. Frey and C. Pulak, *IJNA* 13, 4 (1984), 271–9.
64 F. Fischer, *Die hethitische Keramik von Boğazköy* (1963), 32.
65 C. A. Burney and D. M. Lang, *The Peoples of the Hills* (1971), 47, 86.
66 J. Mellaart, *AnSt* V (1955), 53. The suggestion is made for south-western pottery, but is equally apt for north-western vessels.
67 R. T. Murchese, *AJA* 80 (1976), 410–11.
68 Final publication of the LBA material from Beycesultan is now in hand. In the meantime see *AnSt* V (1955), 39 ff.; VI (1956), 101 ff.; VIII (1958), 93 ff.
69 The suggestion made by the author (*AnSt* IX, 1959, 180) that the writing [D]IŠKUR-*unnaš* represents *šiunaš* (i.e. that the Hittite name of the 'Weather-god' is cognate with Greek Zeus, Latin Iuppiter etc.) can no longer be sustained, for, as pointed out by E. Neu (*Der Anitta-Text*, 1974, 122) the early form of the nominative is *šiuš*, not *šiunaš*. However an alternative suggestion made by Neu, and also by S. R. Bin-Nun (*The Tawananna in the Hittite Kingdom*, 1975, 149 ff.), and supported by O. R. Gurney (*Some Aspects of Hittite Religion*, 1977, 10), that the Indo-European sky-god appears in Hittite

texts as a sun-god ([D]UTU-*uš*) does not seem to the author to carry conviction. It is based on the mention of three deities (Throne-goddess, Weather-god and *šiuš*) in the Anittas-text, and of three deities (Throne-goddess, Weather-god and Sun-god) in another early text which describes the ritual for the erection of a palace. But the equation of *šiuš* and the Sun-god is not as straightforward as it seems. It is for instance possible to interpret the passage in the Anittas-text (lines 10–12) as indicating that the Sun-god was a supporter of rebel lands, which *šiuš* certainly was not, and the introductory passage (lines 1–4) clearly states that the patron deity of Anittas was the Weather-god of Heaven. The triad in the Anittas-text may well be an illusion.
70 For a critical approach to this 'classic view' of Anatolian religious development see D. H. French in *Studien zur Religion und Kultur Kleinasiens* (Festschrift Dörner) (1978), 375–83.
71 The building has been taken to be a scribal school because of the large number of tablet-fragments found there. It has also been suggested that the building was a *halentuwa*-house, where the king and queen changed into ritual dress before entering the precinct for ceremonial purposes (K. Bittel, *AJA* 80, 1976, 70–71).
72 K. Bittel, *Hattusha, Capital of the Hittites* (1970), 107–8.
73 K. Bittel, ibid, 110.
74 P. Neve, *AA* 1982, 389–92. The suggestion of a connection with Yazılıkaya is made because a figure from the female procession has been found near the same village. See H. G. Güterbock, *Belleten* 11 (1947), 189–95; K. Bittel and others, *Yazılıkaya* (1975), 170.
75 O. R. Gurney, *The Hittites*[3] (1980), 166 ff.
76 G. Daux, *BCH* XCIII (1968), 1038 (Argos). Cremation-burial is also attested in the Middle Bronze Age in Epirus (N. G. L. Hammond, *Epirus*, 1967, 229), and in the early Bronze Age on Leukas (W. Dörpfeld, *Alt-Ithaka*, 1927; J. L. Caskey, *CAH*[3] I, 2, 792–3.
77 P. Neve, *AA* 1983, 438.
78 S. Lloyd, *Early Highland Peoples of Anatolia* (1967), 64–5.
79 K. Bittel, *Hattusha, Capital of the Hittites* (1970), 98. This assumption of theological daring is based on the interpretation of the two bulls as being Sheri and Hurri, companions of Teshub. An alternative theory (E. Laroche, *Syria* 40, 1963, 285 f.) makes both bulls representations of Sharruma, son of Teshub and Hebat. This of course does not affect the

artistic unity of the scene, created by the combination of antithetical and overlapping figures.

80 K. Bittel (*Die Hethiter*, 1976, 205–8) may well be right in taking the Alaca sculptures to be a century or more earlier than those at Yazılıkaya. This would certainly help to explain the many differences between the two groups.

81 It may be worthwhile to mention here a passage which has been taken to be a possible second-millennium western Anatolian ancestor of the *Iliad*. It occurs in a Hittite ritual text (KBo IV, 11) in which various ceremonies take place and various narratives are recited by the officiating priest. Only the opening words of the narratives (which are in Luwian) are given; and in one case (line 46) these words *may* be translated 'When they came from steep Wilusa'. Now Wilusa has in the past often been equated (wrongly, in the author's opinion) with Homeric Ilium, and 'steep' is an epithet used by Homer to describe that town. So it is possible to see the phrase, and therefore the text of which it was the

first words, as forming part of a 'Wilusiad', a Bronze Age Luwian epic dealing with the Siege of Troy. Unfortunately there are problems (there always are!). The meaning of the Luwian adjective translated 'steep' is in fact extremely uncertain, and although the noun clearly means *from* somewhere or something, there is no 'determinative' attached to the name in the text to show that it is necessarily the name of a town. Thus the Luwian epic has for the moment to remain only a remote possibility, not so much a Wilusiad as a Will-o'-the-wisp-iad.

82 This is not of course to maintain that any Hittite text is a 'history' in the Classical or modern sense, or that any Hittite text helps to explain the rise of historiography in Ionia, or even that the Hittites were unique in using the past in the ways they did (see for instance J. Van Seters, *In Search of History*, 1983, 100–26). The point is merely that the search for historical 'causes' did not begin with Herodotus.

83 R. S. Young, *AJA* 62 (1958), 139 ff.

84 L. H. Jeffery, *CAH³* III, 1, 832.

Sources of illustrations

Ankara, Archaeological Museum: *Frontispiece*, 7, 9, 10, 11, 32, 36, 77, 84, 86, 87, 89, 91, 93, 94, 95, 125, 131, 132, 136, 137, 139, 140, 141, 142, 143; George Bass 76; Berlin, Deutsches Archäologisches Institut 53, 85; Staatliche Museen zu Berlin 144; Cincinnati Archaeological Expedition 16; Pandora Hay 38; Hirmer Fotoarchiv 14, 15, 23, 24, 36, 48, 79, 87, 97, 104, 105, 113, 115, 116, 117, 120, 121, 127, 129, 130, 131, 132, 133, 136, 137, 138, 139, 140, 141; Istanbul, Archaeological Museum 16; Edmund Lee 40, 47, 70; Seton Lloyd 50, 64, 66; London, Turkish Tourist Board 126; J. Macqueen 43, 68; T. Özgüç₂ 7, 11; Josephine Powell 9, 10, 32, 91; Princeton University Press 42, 45, 46, 67, 81, 82, 123, 146, *Univers des Formes*: 1, 77, 95, 101, 119, 125, 128, 134, 143; K. Bittel, 'Tonschale mit Ritzzeichnung von Boğazköy', *Revue Archéologique*, 1976 Vol. I, 34; from J. Garstang, *Prehistoric Mersin*, 1953, 31, 75; from H. Z. Kosay and M. Akok, *Ausgrabungen von Alaca Höyük 1940–1948*, 1966, 59; from N. Özgüç₂, *The Anatolian Group of Cylinder Impressions from Kültepe*, 1965, 96; from G. Perrot, *Exploration Archéologique de la Galatie*, Vol. I 1862, 13; from Y. Yadin, *Art of Warfare in Biblical Lands*, 1963, 25, 28.

Select bibliography

This is not intended to be an exhaustive bibliography of Hittite studies, but rather an introductory selection of books and articles dealing with subjects and problems mentioned in the text. Many of the works mentioned contain further bibliographies which should be consulted by anyone who wishes to go into greater detail or make up his or her own mind on controversial points.

Abbreviations

AA	*Archäologischer Anzeiger*	*JKlF*	*Jahrbuch für Kleinasiatische*
AfO	*Archiv für Orientforschung*		*Forschung*
AJA	*American Journal of Archaeology*	*JNES*	*Journal of Near Eastern Studies*
AnSt	*Anatolian Studies*	*KBo*	*Keilschrifttexte aus Boghazköi*
Bell	Türk Tarih Kurumu: *Belleten*	*KUB*	*Keilschrifturkunden aus Boghazköi*
BMQ	*British Museum Quarterly*	*MDOG*	*Mitteilungen der deutschen Orient-*
CAH	*Cambridge Ancient History*		*gesellschaft*
IJNA	*International Journal of Nautical*	*OLZ*	*Orientalistische Literaturzeitung*
	Archaeology and Underwater	*RA*	*Revue Archéologique*
	Exploration	*RHA*	*Revue Hittite et Asianique*
ILN	*Illustrated London News*	*ScAm*	*Scientific American*
Ist Mitt	*Istanbuler Mitteilungen*	*SMEA*	*Studi Micenei ed Egeo-Anatolici*
JAOS	*Journal of the American Oriental*	*TAD*	*Türk Arkeoloji Dergisi*
	Society	*TTKR*	*Türk Tarih Kurumu Rapolari*
JCS	*Journal of Cuneiform Studies*	*ZA*	*Zeitschrift für Assyriologie*
JIES	*Journal of Indo-European Studies*		

General

AKURGAL, E. *Ancient Civilizations and Ruins of Turkey*. Istanbul, 1970.

ALKIM, U. B. *Anatolia* I. London, 1969.

BITTEL, K. *Hattusha, Capital of the Hittites*. New York, 1970.

Cambridge Ancient History, 3rd edn, Cambridge, Vol. I, 1 1970; Vol. I, 2 1971; Vol. II, 1 1973; Vol. II, 2 1975.

GOETZE, A. *Kleinasien*. 2nd edn, Munich, 1957.

GURNEY, O. R. *The Hittites*. Harmondsworth and San Francisco, 1952 and subsequent editions. Important changes have been made in the 1980 edition.

LLOYD, S. *Early Anatolia*. Harmondsworth, 1956.

—— *Early Highland Peoples of Anatolia*. London and New York, 1967.

MELLAART, J. *The Archaeology of Ancient Turkey*. London, 1978.

OTTEN, H. 'Das Hethiterreich', in Schmökel, H.

Kulturgeschichte des alten Orient. Stuttgart, 1961.

PRITCHARD, J. B. (ed.) *Ancient Near Eastern Texts Relating to the Old Testament*. Princeton, 1950, 1955, 1969.

SCHMÖKEL, H. *Geschichte des alten Vorderasien*, pp. 119–70. Leiden, 1957.

WALSER G. (ed.) *Neuere Hethiterforschung (Historia: Einzelschriften 7)*. Wiesbaden, 1964.

Summaries of archaeological work and preliminary reports of excavations appear in the Reports of the Annual Excavations Symposium (Kazı Sonuclari Toplantisi), Ankara, 1980–, and in *AJA, AnSt, TAD, TTKR, Bell, MDOG, Orientalia, Anatolica, Anadolu* (Anatolia), *Jahrbericht Ex Oriente Lux*. Many other periodicals (e.g. *RHA, JAOS, JCS, JIES, JNES, ZA*) contain articles dealing with Anatolian topics. An important new source of reference is the

Newsletter for Anatolian Studies, edited by B. J. Collins and published (1985–) by Yale University. Up-to-date editions of texts appear in the two series *Studien zu den Boğazköy Texten* (Wiesbaden, 1965–) and *Texte der Hethiter* (Heidelberg, 1971–).

Chapter 1

ARIK, R. O. *Les Fouilles d' Alaca Höyük, 1935*. Ankara, 1936.

BRICE, W. C. *South-West Asia*. London, 1966. Vol. 8 in Systematic Regional Geography Series, ed. J. F. Unstead. (Excellent on geography of Turkey.)

—— (ed.) *The Environmental History of the Near and Middle East since the Last Ice Age*. London and New York, 1978.

BURNEY, C. A. and LANG, D. M. *The Peoples of the Hills; Ancient Ararat and Caucasus*. London and New York, 1971.

CAMBEL, H. and BRAIDWOOD, R. J. An Early Farming Village in Turkey. *ScAm* March 1970, 50–6.

COHEN, H. 'The Palaeoecology of South Central Anatolia at the End of the Pleistocene and the Beginning of the Holocene.' *AnSt* XX (1970), 119–37.

DEWDNEY, J. C. *Turkey*. London, 1971.

FORBES, R. J. *Studies in Ancient Technology, VIII–IX. (Metallurgy in Antiquity)*. Leiden, 1964.

GARELLI, P. *Les Assyriens en Cappadoce*. Paris, 1963.

GARSTANG, J. *Prehistoric Mersin*. Oxford and New York, 1953.

GÜTERBOCK, H. G. 'Die historische Tradition und ihre literarische Gestaltung bei Babyloniern und Hethitern bis 1200'. *ZA* 42 (1934), 1 ff., and 44 (1938), 45 ff.

—— 'Kaneš and Neša, Two Forms of One Anatolian Name'. *Eretz-Israel* V, (1958), 46–50.

KOŞAY, H. Z. *Ausgrabungen von Alaca Höyük*. Ankara, 1944.

—— *Les Fouilles d'Alaca Höyük, 1937–39*. Ankara, 1951.

LARSEN, M. T. *The Old Assyrian City-State and its Colonies*. Copenhagen, 1976.

LLOYD, S. and MELLAART, J. *Beycesultan*. London, Vol. I, 1962; Vol. II, 1965.

MELLAART, J. *Çatal Hüyük. A Neolithic Town in Anatolia*. London and New York, 1967.

—— *The Chalcolithic and Early Bronze Ages in the Near East and Anatolia*. Beirut, 1966.

—— *Earliest Civilizations of the Near East*. London and New York, 1965.

—— 'Excavations at Çatal Hüyük'. *AnSt* XII (1962), 41–65; XIII (1963), 43–103; XIV (1964), 39–119; XVI (1966), 165–91.

—— *Hacilar*. Edinburgh, 1970.

—— *The Neolithic of the Near East*. London, 1975.

ORLIN, L. L. *Assyrian Colonies in Cappodocia*. The Hague, 1970.

OTTEN, H. 'Zu den Anfangen der Hethitischen Geschichte'. *MDOG* 83 (1951), 33–45.

ÖZGÜÇ, N. *The Anatolian Group of Cylinder Impressions from Kültepe*. Ankara, 1965.

—— 'Marble Idols and Statuettes from the Excavations at Kültepe'. *Bell* XXI (1957), 71–80.

ÖZGÜÇ, T. 'The Art and Architecture of Ancient Kanesh'. *Anatolia* VIII (1964), 27–48.

—— 'An Assyrian Trading Outpost'. *ScAm* Feb. 1963, 97–106.

—— *Ausgrabungen in Kültepe, 1948*. Ankara, 1950.

—— 'The Dagger of Anitta'. *Bell* XX (1956), 33–36.

—— *Kültepe-Kaniş; New Researches at the Center of the Assyrian Trade Colonies*. Ankara, 1959.

ÖZGÜÇ, T. and N. *Ausgrabungen in Kültepe, 1949*. Ankara, 1953.

REDMAN, C. L. *The Rise of Civilization*. San Francisco, 1978.

SCHLIEMANN, H. *Troy and its Remains*. London, 1875.

—— *Ilios the City of the Trojans*. London and New York, 1880.

—— *Troja: Results of the Latest Researches and Discoveries on the Site of Homer's Troy*. London and New York, 1884.

TODD, I. A. 'Aşıklı Hüyük'. *AnSt* XVI (1966), 139–63.

TODD, I. A. and PASQUARE, G. 'The Chipped Stone industry of Avla Dağ. *AnSt* XV (1965), 95–112.

UCKO, P. J. and DIMBLEBY, G. W. (eds). *The Domestication and Exploitation of Plants and Animals*. London and Chicago, 1969.

Chapter 2

CROSSLAND, R. A. 'Immigrants from the North'. *CAH*³ I, 2, 824 ff.

CROSSLAND, R. A. and BIRCHALL, A. *Bronze Age Migrations in the Aegean*. London and Park Ridge, 1973 and 1974.

FRENCH, D. H. 'Prehistoric Sites in N-W Anatolia'. *AnSt* XVII (1967), esp. 61–4.

FRIEDRICH, J. *Hethitisches Elementarbuch* I–II. Heidelberg, 1946–60.
—— *Hethitisches Keilschriftlesebuch.* Heidelberg, 1960.
—— *Hethitisches Wörterbuch.* Heidelberg, 1952 and supplements. A second edition, by Friedrich and A. Kammenhuber, began publication in 1975.
GIMBUTAS, M. 'The Indo-Europeans: Archaeological Problems'. *American Anthropologist* 65 (1963), 815 ff.
—— 'Proto-Indo-European Culture', in *Indo-European and Indo-Europeans.* Philadelphia, 1970.
GÜTERBOCK, H. G. and HOFFNER, H. A. (eds.). *Chicago Hittite Dictionary.* Chicago, 1980–.
HROZNÝ, B. *Die Lösung des Hethitischen Problems.* Leipzig, 1915.
—— *Die Sprache der Hethiter*, Leipzig, 1917.
KNUDTZON, J. A. *Die zwei Arzawa-Briefe: die ältesten Urkunden in indo-germanischer Sprache.* Leipzig, 1902.
LAROCHE, E. *Dictionnaire de la Langue Louvite.* Paris, 1959.
—— *Les Hiéroglyphes Hittites*, Vol. I. Paris, 1960.
MACQUEEN, J. G. 'The First Arrival of Indo-European Elements in Greece. Some Observations from Anatolia', in *Acta of the 2nd International Colloquium on Aegean Prehistory.* Athens, 1972.
MELLAART, J. 'Anatolia and the Indo-Europeans', in *JIES* 9 (1981), 135–49.
—— 'The End of the Early Bronze Age in Anatolia and the Aegean'. *AJA* 62 (1958), 9–33.
MELLINK, M. J. 'Anatolian Chronology', in Ehrich, R. W. (ed.) *Chronologies in Old World Archaeology.* Chicago, 1965.
PALMER, L. R. *Mycenaeans and Minoans.* London and New York, 1965.
PUHVEL, J. *Hittite Etymological Dictionary.* Berlin, Amsterdam, New York, 1984– .
SAYCE, A. H. 'On the Hamathite Inscriptions'. *Transactions of the Society for Biblical Archaeology*, V. 1877.
—— 'The Hittites in Asia Minor'. *Academy*, Aug. 16, 1879.
—— 'The Monuments of the Hittites'. *Transactions of the Society for Biblical Archaeology*, VII. 1882.
STURTEVANT, E. H. *A Comparative Grammar of the Hittite Language.* 2nd edn Philadelphia, 1951.
—— *A Hittite Chrestomathy.* Philadelphia, 1935.

Chapter 3

ASTOUR M. C. 'New Evidence on the Last Days of Ugarit', in *AJA* 69 (1965), 253–258.
BIN-NUN, S. R. *The Tawananna in the Hittite Kingdom.* Heidelberg, 1975.
BRYCE, T. R. 'The Lukka Problem – and a Possible Solution' in *JNES* 33 (1974), 395–404.
—— *The Major Historical Texts of Early Hittite History.* Queensland, 1982.
—— 'The Role of the Lukka People in Late Bronze Age Anatolia', in *Antichthon* 13 (1979), 1–11.
—— 'Some Geographical and Political Aspects of Mursilis' Arzawa Campaign', in *AnSt* XXIV (1974), 103–16.
FORRER, E. O. 'Die Griechen in den Boghazköi-Texten'. *OLZ* 1924, 113–18.
—— Vorhomerische Griechen in den Keilschrifttexten von Boghazköi. *MDOG* 63 (1924), 1–22.
FOXHALL, L. and DAVIES, J. K. (eds.). *The Trojan War: its Historicity and Context.* Bristol, 1984.
FRANKLIN, A. D., OLIN, J. S. and WERTIME, T. H. (eds.). *The Search for Ancient Tin.* Washington D.C., 1978.
GARSTANG, J. and GURNEY, O. R. *The Geography of the Hittite Empire*, London, 1959.
GILES, D. L. and KUIJPERS, E. Stratiform Copper Deposit, Northern Anatolia, Turkey: Evidence for Early Bronze I (2800 BC) Mining Activity, in *Science* 186 (29/11/74), 823–5.
GOETZE, A. *Die Annalen des Mursilis.* Leipzig, 1933.
—— *Hattusilis.* Leipzig, 1925.
—— *Hattusilis. Neue Bruchstücke.* Leipzig, 1930.
—— *Madduwattaš.* Leipzig, 1928.
—— 'The Roads of Northern Cappadocia in Hittite Times'. *RHA* 61 (1957), 91 ff.
GURNEY, O. R. *The Hittite Empire* in LARSEN, M. T. (ed.). *Power and Propaganda: a Symposium on Ancient Empires.* Copenhagen, 1979.
GÜTERBOCK, H. G. 'The Ahhiyawa Problem Reconsidered', in *AJA* 87 (1983), 133–8.
—— 'The Deeds of Suppiluliuma, as Told by his Son Mursili II'. *JCS* 10 (1956), 41 ff.
—— 'The Hittite Conquest of Cyprus Reconsidered'. *JNES* 26 (1967), 73–81.
—— The North-Central Area of Hittite Anatolia. *JNES* 20 (1961), 88 ff.
HANKEY, V. 'Turmoil in the Near East *c.* 1200 BC', in *Asian Affairs* V (1974), 51–9.

HAUSCHILD, R. *Die indogermanischer Völker und Sprachen Kleinasiens.* Berlin, 1964.

HEINHOLD-KRAHMER, S. *Arzawa: Untersuchungen zu seiner Geschichte nach den hethitischen Quellen.* Heidelberg, 1977.

HODDINOTT, R. F. *The Thracians.* London, 1981.

HOUWINK TEN CATE, P. H. J. *The Records of the Early Hittite Empire.* Leiden, 1970.

HUXLEY, G. L. *Achaeans and Hittites.* Oxford, 1960.

JESUS, P. S. DE *The Development of Prehistoric Mining and Metallurgy in Anatolia.* Oxford, 1980.

—— 'Metal Resources in Ancient Anatolia', in *AnSt* XXVIII (1978), 97–102.

—— 'A Survey of Some Ancient Mines and Smelting Sites', in *Archäologie und Naturwissenschaften* 2 (1981), 95–105.

JEWELL, E. R. *The Archaeology and History of Western Anatolia during the Second Millennium* BC. Dissertation, University of Pennsylvania, 1974.

KITCHEN, K. A. *Suppiluliuma and the Amarna Pharaohs.* Liverpool, 1962.

—— Review of Wente E. and Johnson J. (eds). 'Studies in Honour of G. R. Hughes', in *Serapis* 4 (1977–8), 66–78.

KOŠAK, S. 'Western Neighbours of the Hittites', in *Eretz-Israel* XV (1981), 12–16.

LAROCHE, E. *Catalogue des Textes Hittites.* Paris, 1971.

LUCKENBILL, D. D. *Ancient Records of Assyria and Babylonia* II. Chicago 1927.

MACQUEEN, J. G. 'Geography and History in Western Asia Minor in the Second Millennium B.C.' *AnSt* XVIII (1968), 169 ff.

MEE, C. 'Aegean Trade and Settlement in Anatolia in the Second Millennium BC', in *AnSt* XXVIII (1978), 121–55.

MELLAART, J. 'Anatolian Trade with Europe and Anatolian Geography and Culture Provinces in the Late Bronze Age'. *AnSt* XVIII (1968), 187 ff.

—— 'Western Anatolia, Beycesultan and the Hittites', in *Mansel'e Armağan* (*Melanges Mansel*), Ankara, 1974, 493–526.

MELLINK, M. J. 'Archaeological Comments on Ahhiyawa-Achaeans in Western Anatolia', in *AJA* 87 (1983), 138–41.

MUHLY, J. D. *Copper and Tin.* New Haven, Conn., 1973–6.

—— 'Hittites and Achaeans: Ahhiyawa Redomitus', in *Historia* 23 (1974), 129–45.

—— 'The Hittites and the Aegean World', in *Expedition* 16, 2 (Winter 1974), 3–10.

—— 'Sources of Tin and the Beginnings of Bronze Metallurgy', in *AJA* 89 (1985), 275–91.

NEU, E. *Der Anitta-Text.* Wiesbaden, 1974.

OTTEN, H. *Eine althethitische Erzählung um die Stadt Zalpa.* Wiesbaden, 1973.

—— 'Neue Quellen zum Ausklang der Hethitischen Geschichte'. *MDOG* 94 (1963), 1–23.

—— *MDOG* 91 (1958), 75–84. (Historical text of Hattusilis I.)

ÖZGÜÇ, T. *Excavations at Maşat Höyük and Investigations in its Vicinity.* Ankara, 1978.

PAGE, D. L. *History and the Homeric Iliad.* Berkeley, 1959.

RAPP, G. and GIFFORD, T. A. *Troy: The Archaeological Geology.* Princeton, 1982.

RYAN, C. W. *A Guide to the Known Minerals of Turkey.* Ankara, 1960.

SANDARS, N. K. *The Sea Peoples.* London, 1985.

SCHULER, E. VON. *Die Kaškäer: Ein Beitrag zur Ethnographie des alten Kleinasien.* Berlin, 1965.

SINGER, I. 'Hittites and Hattians in Anatolia at the Beginning of the Second Millennium BC', in *JIES* 9 (1981), 119–34.

—— 'Western Anatolia in the Thirteenth Century BC according to the Hittite Sources', in *AnSt* XXXIII (1983), 205–17.

SOMMER, F. *Die Ahhijavā-Urkunden.* Munich, 1932.

STEINER, G. 'Die Ahhiyawa-Frage heute', in *Saeculum* 15 (1964), 365–92.

—— 'The Role of the Hittites in Ancient Anatolia', in *JIES* 9 (1981), 150–73.

WERTIME, T. A. and MUHLY, J. D. (eds). *The Coming of the Age of Iron.* New Haven and London, 1980.

YAKAR, J. 'Hittite Involvement in Western Anatolia', in *AnSt* XXVI (1976), 117–28.

—— 'The Indo-Europeans and their Impact on Anatolian Cultural Development', in *JIES* 9 (1981), 94–112.

—— 'Recent Contributions to the Historical Geography of the Hittite Empire', in *MDOG* 112 (1980), 75–94.

Chapter 4

BITTEL, K. 'Fragment einer Hethitischen Reliefscherbe mit Wagendarstellung', in *Studien zur Religion und Kultur Kleinasiens* (*Festschrift Dörner*), 1978, 178–82.

—— 'Tonschale mit Ritzzeichnung von Boğazköy', in *RA*, 1976, 9–14.

GOETZE, A. 'Warfare in Asia Minor'. *Iraq* 25 (1963), 124 ff.

MAXWELL-HYSLOP, R. 'Daggers and Swords in Western Asia'. *Iraq* VIII (1946), 1–65.
—— 'Western Asiatic Shaft-Hole Axes'. *Iraq* XI (1949), 90–129.
OSTEN, H. H. VON DER. *The Alishar Huyuk. Seasons of 1930–32*, Part II. Chicago, 1937.
PUCHSTEIN, O. *Boghasköi, Die Bauwerke.* Leipzig, 1912.
STRONACH, D. 'The Development and Diffusion of Metal Types in Early Bronze Age Anatolia'. *AnSt* VII (1957), 89–125.
YADIN, Y. *The Art of Warfare in Biblical Lands.* London, 1963.

Chapter 5

FRIEDRICH, J. *Die hethitischen Gesetze.* Leiden, 1959.
—— *Staatsvertrage des Hatti-Reiches in Hethitischer Sprache.* Leipzig, 1926–30.
GURNEY, O. R. 'Hittite Kingship', in Hooke, S. H. (ed.), *Myth, Ritual and Kingship.* Oxford and New York, 1958.
GÜTERBOCK, H. G. 'Authority and Law in the Hittite Kingdom'. *JAOS* Suppl. 17 (1954), 16–24.
PIERCE, J. E. *Life in a Turkish Village.* New York, 1964.
SCHULER, E. VON. Hethitische Dienstanweisungen für Hof- und Statts-beamte'. *AfO*, Beiheft 10, 1957.
STIRLING, P. *Turkish Village.* London, 1965.
WEIDNER, E. F. *Politische Dokumente aus Kleinasien.* Leipzig, 1923.

Chapter 6

BASS, G. *Cape Gelidonya: a Bronze Age Shipwreck.* Philadelphia, 1967.
—— 'Sheytan Deresi: Preliminary Report', in *IJNA* 5 (1976), 293–303.
——, FREY, D. A. and PULAK, C. 'A Late Bronze Age Shipwreck at Kaş, Turkey', in *IJNA* 13 (1984), 271–9.
BERAN, T. *Die hethitische Glyptik von Boğazköy.* Berlin, 1967.
BITTEL, K. and GÜTERBOCK, H. G. *Boğazköy. Neue Untersuchungen in der Hethitischen Hauptstadt.* Berlin, 1935.
BITTEL, K. and NAUMANN, R. *Boğazköy II. Neue Untersuchungen hethitischer Architektur.* Berlin, 1938.
—— *Boğazköy-Hattusa I. Architektur, Topographie, Landeskunde u. Siedlungsgeschichte.* Stuttgart, 1952.

BITTEL, K., NAUMANN, R. *et al. Boğazköy III. Funde aus den Grabungen 1952–55.* Berlin, 1957.
BLEGEN, C. W. *et al. Troy.* Princeton, Vol. III, 1953; Vol. IV, 1958.
BOEHMER, R. M. *Die Kleinfunde von Boğazköy.* Berlin, 1972.
—— *Die Kleinfunde aus der Unterstadt von Boğazköy.* Berlin, 1979.
—— *Die Reliefkeramik von Boğazköy.* Berlin, 1983.
BURNEY, C. A. 'Northern Anatolia before Classical Times'. *AnSt* VI (1956), 179 ff.
DRIESCH, A. VON DEN, and BOESSNECK, J. *Reste von Haus und Jagdtieren aus der Unterstadt von Boğazköy-Hattuşa.* Berlin, 1981.
FISCHER, F. *Die hethitische Keramik von Boğazköy.* Berlin, 1963.
FRENCH, D. H. 'Prehistoric Sites in N-W Anatolia'. I *AnSt* XVII (1967), 49–100; II *AnSt* XIX (1969), 41–98.
GOETZE, A. 'Hittite Dress'. *Corolla Linguistica.* Wiesbaden, 1955.
GOLDMAN, H. *Excavations at Gözlü Kule, Tarsus,* II. Princeton, 1956.
GÜTERBOCK, H. G. *Siegel aus Boğazköy.* Berlin, Vol. I 1940; Vol. II 1942.
HOFFNER, H. A. *Alimenta Hethaeorum.* New Haven, 1974.
KADISH, B. 'Excavation of Prehistoric Remains at Aphrodisias, 1967', in *AJA* 73 (1969), 49–65.
—— 'Excavation of the Prehistoric Remains at Aphrodisias: 1968 and 1969', in *AJA* 75 (1971), 121–40.
KOŞAY, H. A. and AKOK, M. *Ausgrabungen von Alaca Höyük 1940–1948.* Ankara, 1966.
LAMB, W. 'Excavations at Kusura near Afyon Karahisar'. *Archaeologia* 86 (1936) 1–64; 87 (1937), 217–74.
—— *Excavations at Thermi in Lesbos.* Cambridge and New York, 1936.
LLOYD, S. *Beycesultan* III, i. London, 1972
LLOYD, S. and MELLAART, J. 'Beycesultan Excavations; First Preliminary Report. *AnSt* V (1955), 39–93. Second Preliminary Report. *AnSt* VI (1956), 101–35.
LOON, M. N. VAN. *Korucutepe I–III.* Amsterdam, 1975–80.
MARCHESE, R. T. 'Report on the West Acropolis Excavation at Aphrodisias: 1971–1973', in *AJA* 80 (1976), 393–413.
MAXWELL-HYSLOP, R. *Western Asiatic Jewellery c. 3000–612 B.C.* London and New York, 1971.

MELLAART, J. 'The Second Millennium Chronology of Beycesultan'. *AnSt* XX (1970), 55–67.

Middle East Technical University. Keban Project Reports. I–. 1968–.

NAUMANN, R. *Architektur Kleinasiens*. 2nd edn. Tübingen, 1971.

NEVE, P. 'Annual reports on Boğazköy', in *AA* from 1979 onwards.

—— *Büyükkale. Die Bauwerke*. Berlin, 1982.

ORTHMANN, W. *Frühe Keramik von Boğazköy*. Berlin, 1963.

ÖZGÜÇ, T. 'The Bitik Vase', *Anatolia* II (1957), 57–78.

—— 'New Finds from Horoztepe', *Anatolia* VIII (1964), 1 ff.

ÖZGÜÇ, T. and N. *Ausgrabungen in Karahüyük 1947*. Ankara, 1949.

SCHAEFFER, C. F. A. *et al*. *Ugaritica* III. Paris, 1956.

SCHIRMER, W. *Die Bebauung am unteren Büyükkale-Nordwesthang in Boğazköy*. Berlin, 1969.

SEIDL, U. *Gefässmarken von Boğazköy*. Berlin, 1972.

Chapter 7

BITTEL, K. *et. al. Boğazköy-Hattusa IX. Das hethitische Felsheiligtum Yazılıkaya*. Berlin, 1975.

—— *Die hethitischen Grabfunde von Osmankayasi*. Berlin, 1958.

DEIGHTON, H. J. *The 'Weather-god' in Hittite Anatolia*. Oxford, 1982.

EMRE, K. *Yanarlar. A Hittite cemetery near Afyon*. Ankara, 1978.

GURNEY, O. R. 'Hittite Prayers of Mursili II'. *Annals of Archaeology and Anthropology* 27. Liverpool, 1940.

—— *Some Aspects of Hittite Religion*. Oxford, 1977.

GÜTERBOCK, H. G. 'Hittite Religion', in Ferm, V., *Forgotten Religions*. New York, 1949.

—— 'An Outline of the Hittite AN.TAH.ŠUM Festival'. *JNES* XIX (1960), 80 ff.

HAAS, V. *Der Kult von Nerik*. Rome, 1970.

LAROCHE, E. 'Le Panthéon de Yazılıkaya'. *JCS* VI (1952), 114–23.

—— *Textes Mythologiques Hittites en Transcription*. Paris, 1965.

LEBRUN, R. *Hymnes et Prières Hittites*. Louvain-la-Neuve, 1980.

MACQUEEN, J. G. 'Hattian Mythology and Hittite Monarchy'. *AnSt* IX (1959), 171–88.

MELLINK, M. J. *A Hittite Cemetery at Gordion*. Philadelphia, 1956.

ORTHMANN, W. *Das Gräberfeld bei Ilıca*. Wiesbaden, 1967.

OTTEN, H. *Hethitische Totenrituale*. Berlin, 1958.

SINGER, I. *The Hittite KI.LAM Festival*. Wiesbaden, 1983–4.

Chapter 8

AKURGAL, E. *The Art of the Hittites*, London and New York, 1962.

ARTS COUNCIL. *Hittite Art and the Antiquities of Anatolia*. London, 1964.

BITTEL, K. *Die Hethiter. Die Kunst Anatoliens vom Ende des 3 bis zum Anfang des 1 Jahrtausends vor Christus*. Munich, 1976.

BOSSERT, H. T. *Altanatolien*. Berlin, 1942.

FRANKFORT H. A. *The Art and Architecture of the Ancient Orient*. 4th edn. Harmondsworth, 1970.

GÜTERBOCK, H. G. 'The Composition of Hittite Prayers to the Sun'. *JAOS* 78 (1958), 237 ff.

—— 'Hittite Mythology', in Kramer, S. N. (ed.), *Mythologies of the Ancient World*. New York, 1961.

—— 'The Hittite Version of the Hurrian Kumarbi Myths; Oriental Forerunners of Hesiod'. *AJA* 52 (1948), 123 ff.

—— 'Notes on some Hittite Monuments'. *AnSt* VI (1956), 53 ff.

—— *The Song of Ullikummi*. New Haven, 1952.

MCNEILL, I. 'The Metre of the Hittite Epic'. *AnSt* XIII (1963), 237 ff.

RIEMSCHNEIDER, M. *Die Welt der Hethiter*. 5th edn. Stuttgart, 1965.

VIEYRA, M. *Hittite Art, 2300–750 B.C.* London and Hollywood-by-the-sea, 1955.

Chapter 9

AKURGAL, E. *Phrygische Kunst*. Ankara, 1955.

ASTOUR, M. C. *Hellenosemitica*. Leiden, 1965.

HAWKINS, J. D. 'The Neo-Hittite States in Syria and Anatolia', in *CAH²* III, 1, 372–441.

HOUWINK TEN CATE, P. H. J. *Kleinasien zwischen Hethitern und Persern*. Frankfurt, 1967.

—— *The Luwian Population Groups of Lycia and Cilicia Aspera during the Hellenistic Period*. Leiden, 1961.

NEUMANN, G. *Untersuchungen zum Weiterleben hethitischen u. luwischen Sprachgutes in hellenistischer u. römischer Zeit*. Wiesbaden, 1961.

YOUNG, R. S. 'Reports on Gordion excavations', in *AJA* 59 (1955) and subsequent volumes.

Index